AERODATA INTERNATIONAL

U.S. Navy Carrier Fighters Of World War II

F2A Buffalo • F4F Wildcat • F6F Hellcat
F4U Corsair • F8F Bearcat

squadron/signal publications

Published 1987 by Squadron/Signal Publications, Inc.
1115 Crowley Drive
Carrollton, Texas 75011-5010

ISBN 0-89747-194-6

Printed in Hong Kong
for Imago Productions (F.E.) Pte. Ltd.

BREWSTER F2A BUFFALO

Fig. 1 *A flight of F2A-3s peels off over Florida, 3 August 1942.* (USN-NARS)

The one and only time that Brewster Buffaloes in US markings entered combat with enemy aircraft, they suffered appalling casualties. Nineteen F2A-3s of VMF-221 led by Major Floyd Parks, along with six F4F-3 Wildcats, intercepted a strike force of 108 Japanese aircraft as they approached Midway Island on the morning of 3 June 1942. Unfortunately for the young Marines, the Japanese force included 36 A6M2s which tore into the Buffaloes. The result was a disaster. Thirteen Buffaloes, including that flown by Maj Parks, were downed, and only two of the six that landed back on Sand Island were in fit condition to fly again. These results did not differ much from the outcome of other air combats between the Buffalo and the Japanese. The British, Australians and Dutch had each flown Brewsters against Zeros (and Claudes, as well as Army Oscars and Nates), in the defence of Malaya and the East Indies, and each had suffered similar losses.

The tendency was then, and has been since, to blame the Buffalo for these failures. From 1942 to the present, the Brewster has repeatedly been described as an inadequate fighter flown by brave pilots who deserved a better mount. But a few discordant notes enter into this veritable symphony of bad press. How could pilots such as Flt Lt T A Vigors with two others from 453 Squadron bring down nine Japanese attackers in two separate raids if this fighter was so inadequate? Why did the Finns conduct a four-year love affair with this fighter, during the course of which they scored an incredible average of more than 10 victories per airframe? (Admittedly, a large percentage of this total was accumulated against mediocre opposition, but a fair number of vic-

tories came against fighters such as the LaG-5, Curtiss Tomahawk and Spitfire V.) How could this be the same aircraft? The answer can only be that the Brewster Buffalo (at least in its early form) wasn't nearly as bad as most critics have claimed. It was obsolete in comparison with much of the opposition that it fought, and was almost always outnumbered, but neither of these were the Buffalo's fault. It showed repeatedly that, while never outstanding, in the hands of competent pilots, the Buffalo was a competent fighter.

Many of the Brewster's critics tend to forget when the Buffalo was designed and what its contemporaries looked like. The F2A Buffalo originated in a loose US Navy Request for Proposals issued in early 1935. The Navy has been frequently criticised for entering World War II with largely obsolete equipment, but its 1935 RFP was certainly ambitious enough. The aircraft that it called for would have been superior to any of its shipboard contemporaries and equivalent to most landbased ones. The new aircraft had to achieve a top speed of 300mph (483km/h) with a Wright Cyclone radial of 850hp while having a landing speed of less than 85mph (137km/h). While the RFP did not specify the configuration of the aircraft that the Navy expected, the choice of Brewster's monoplane design on 5 November 1935 indicates that service's acceptance that the day of the biplane was over. The US Navy, along with other navies, disliked monoplanes because of their tendency toward higher landing speeds and reduced manoeuvrability. Just to be safe, it protected itself by also ordering a prototype of the Grumman XF4F-1 biplane at the same time.

Fig. 2 Left, Fig. 3 Above *The XF2A-1 in the air and on the ground. The basic shape is there, but the cowling and tail would be altered as a result of the NACA wind tunnel tests.* (USN-NARS)

The XF2A-1 (Brewster designation – Model B-139, BuNo 0451) first flew in December 1937, the design having been revised to accept a 950hp Wright R-1820-22 driving a three-bladed Hamilton Standard hydromatic propeller. Armament was a .30 calibre and a .50 calibre machine gun in the engine cowling, but space for another .50 calibre gun was provided in each wing. Construction was conventional. The frame was all-metal, covered with flush-rivetted stressed aluminium. Control surfaces were fabric-covered. Advanced design features included split flaps, which allowed an acceptable landing speed, and retracting landing gear. Landing gear retraction was something of a novelty at that time in naval aircraft, the prevailing opinion being that state-of-the-art retraction mechanisms couldn't absorb the stresses of carrier landings. In this case, conventional wisdom proved correct. The Buffalo's landing gear was poorly designed and caused problems throughout the aircraft's service life.

When the XF2A-1 began its trials, the Navy expressed considerable disappointment with the Buffalo's performance. Power from the Wright Cyclone fell off to 750hp at 15,200ft (4328m) and top speed at that altitude was only 277.5mph (447 km/h), considerably below specification. Service ceiling was 30,900ft (9418m) and climb rate was 2750ft/min (838m/min). The stalling speed of 67mph (108km/h) was only 1mph (1.6km/h) higher than that of the F3F, the Navy's then standard biplane fighter, and well within expectations. The other point about which the Navy complained was the Buffalo's lack of wing folding, but it agreed to wait for the expected addition of that feature at a later date.

So disappointed was the Navy in the prototype's performance that it chose a novel expedient. On 21 April 1938, the XF2A-1 was delivered to the NACA's Langley Aeronautical Laboratory. For the first time in the US, an actual aircraft was hoisted into a wind tunnel and subjected to controlled airstream testing. NACA (predecessor to NASA) came up with a series of recommendations for increasing the top speed and resolving some nagging instability problems which had showed up in early flight tests. Redesigning the engine cowling, raising the canopy and increasing the area of the vertical tail all combined to increase stability and add an expected 31mph to the top speed.

The US Navy was now firmly committed to introducing a monoplane fighter into the fleet, but the slow gestation period of the Buffalo and its rival design, the Grumman F4F, meant that the new fighter would no longer be quite so advanced by the time it entered service. (The biplane F4F-1 was never built, and the sole monoplane F4F-2 suffered from even more serious development delays than those that plagued the Buffalo.) Despite its failings, the redesigned XF2A-1 was the best choice available to the Navy, and on 11 June 1938 the Buffalo was accepted and a contract for 55 F2A-1s, powered by the 950hp Wright R-1820-34, was signed. The production fighter was to feature a pair of .50 calibre machine guns in the cowling, increased fuel capacity and a top speed of 301mph (484km/h). The first F2A-1 (Model B-239, BuNo 1386) was delivered in July 1939.

Fig. 4 *The second F2A-1 (BuNo 01387) on exhibition at the New York World's Fair in 1939, one of only 11 completed to this standard. Note the small vertical tail. The markings are those of VF-3's CO's aircraft. All F2A-1s were upgraded to "dash 2" standard before they saw much service with VF-3 on Saratoga. The tail is white; nose, band and wing chevrons are red.* (USN-NARS via Jim Maas)

Fig. 5 *VF-3's CO's Buffalo was another upgraded "dash-1". These 11 aircraft can be distinguished from F2A-2s by their longer nose. Some, like BuNo 1396 seen here, retained their small spinner. The cowling and band are royal red.* (USN via Hal Andrews)

In order to gain a true perspective on the F2A, it is necessary to compare it to its contemporaries. Only two other nations had substantial carrier air forces in the 1930s, Japan and Great Britain. At the time of the Buffalo's introduction, the Japanese fleet was equipped with Mitsubishi A5M4 Claudes. Inferior to the F2A-1 in virtually every respect except manoeuvrability and ceiling, the Claude was a lightly constructed fighter that was neither fast enough to catch a Buffalo nor strong enough to bring one down. The A6M2, which was to be the Buffalo's bane, was still six months away from prototype flight, and a year away from squadron service. Two months prior to delivery of the first F2A-1, the Royal Navy embarked a new fighter, the Gloster Sea Gladiator, a biplane with a top speed of 245mph (394km/h). The F2A-1 was in fact superior to its contemporaries. If it was decimated two and a half years later by aircraft of more recent design, that certainly can't be blamed on the Buffalo. If fault is to be found, it should be with the US Navy for not having a replacement in the works soon enough.

In the event, the US Navy received only 11 F2A-1s (BuNos 1386-96). These were intended for VF-3 on *Saratoga*, but were not taken on strength immediately.

The Navy, even at this point, considered the F2A-1 an interim model to be employed only until more powerful versions became available. The XF2A-1 had crashed in April 1939 as a result of engine failure. When it was rebuilt, it was equipped with an R-1820-40 Cyclone rated at 1200hp, driving a three-bladed electric prop, and was redesignated the XF2A-2 (Model B-339). The new powerplant increased the maximum speed to 324 mph (521km/h) but otherwise had a detrimental effect on handling. The new powerplant was 900lb (408kg) heavier than the engine it replaced, reducing manoeuvrability and lowering the climb rate by over 500ft/min (152m/min). Despite this degradation of overall performance, the higher top speed was very impressive, and the Navy placed an order for 43 F2A-2s in late 1939.

War had meanwhile broken out in Europe and many of the combatant nations looked to the vast underemployed US aviation industry to fill immediate needs. No fewer than four European countries, Finland, Holland, Belgium and Great Britain, placed orders for Brewster Buffaloes in quick succession. The first in line was Finland, which was actively involved in a shooting war with Soviet Russia. American compassion for little

Fig. 6 *The Buffalo prototype (BuNo 0451) was also the XF2A-2 with enlarged tail, revised cowling and more powerful engine. Only the prototype had its radio mast on the port side.* (USN-NARS via Jim Maas)

Fig. 7   *3-F-8 was one of the converted "dash-1s". The bigger spinner and cuffed propeller were characteristic of the F2A-2.*

(USN-NARS via Jim Mass)

Finland and the Navy's desire to build F2A-2s instead of 'dash-1s' fit together neatly. A contract was signed selling the 44 remaining F2A-1s (B-239s, Finnish serial numbers BW-351-394) to the Finns. As delivered, the Finnish Buffaloes were identical to the F2A-1s except that all naval equipment was removed and an export version of the Cyclone, the R-1820-G5, was installed.

As it turned out, the Buffaloes, crated, shipped to Sweden, reassembled and flown to Finland, had only just arrived when peace with Russia was signed on 13 March 1941. The peace proved shortlived, however, and all 44 Buffaloes saw plenty of action in the 'Continuation War' which began with the German invasion of Russia in late June.

Fig. 8   *The life raft housing behind the pilot's headrest and short tail fairing were standard on US Buffaloes. Export versions, which did not need a tailhook, had a longer tailcone.* (USN)

The Finns were the only nation to fly the 'dash-1' in combat and thoroughly appreciated the little fighter. One airframe, BW-393, gained 41 victories. When too few B-239s remained to equip all four flights of LeLv 24, they were transferred to LeLv 26 in spring 1944. They flew with this squadron until Finland again signed a peace treaty with Russia on 4 September 1944 and then flew against the Germans until they were withdrawn from combat in December. Even this wasn't the end of the line for the Finnish Buffaloes which continued in various roles until finally retired in September 1948.

(The Finns were so impressed with the Brewster fighter that they planned to supplement the 44 they bought with up to 90 to be built locally. They were to be built of plywood around a metal frame, powered by captured Russian M-62 radials. Except for a slightly smaller cowling, they would have been externally identical to the B-239. A single damaged Brewster, BW-392, was taken in hand at the Tampere Aircraft Factory and given new plywood wings. Because the plywood wing structure left no room for fuel stowage, three tanks were installed in the fuselage. The performance of the hybrid fighter, dubbed the Humu, proved disappointing, mainly because power fall-off at altitude by the Soviet engine exceeded that of the Cyclone, also because the plywood wings were heavier than the metal originals. Nevertheless, on 16 October 1942 four prototypes were ordered with total production planned to be 90 airframes. Tooling up for production was slow, however,

and when BW-392 crashed on 5 June 1943, enthusiasm for the Humu began to wane. The order was reduced to 55 aircraft in early 1944 and then officially cancelled on 17 June. Work did continue on the one airframe that was nearly complete, HM-671, which finally flew on 8 August 1944. On 1 January 1945, the sole Humu was retired after accumulating only 20 hours of airtime. HM-671 still exists as a museum piece in Finland.)

F2A-2s began to be delivered to the Navy in September 1940, the first ones being converted 'dash-1s' which had only briefly served with VF-3 in their original configuration. That squadron and VF-2 from *Lexington* received their new fighters late in the year. Except for the new engine and propeller, they were essentially identical to the F2A-1. External changes were minimal. The exhaust stub was relocated slightly further up the side of the fuselage and no longer intruded into the rear edge of the cowling, the propeller had cuffed blades and a larger spinner and, finally, a line of vents was introduced in the forward fuselage above the wing leading edge. The last 13 of the 44 new F2A-2s carried .50 calibre machine guns in the wing positions and introduced some pilot armour and self-sealing tanks. This additional weight only served to further degrade performance. By November, VF-2 reported 17 F2A-2s on strength, while VF-3 had 15. These 'dash-2s' were destined never to see combat. VF-3 traded its Buffaloes for Wildcats during late 1941, while VF-2 took on F2A-3s in the place of its F2A-2s in September of that year.

Fig. 9 *BW-378, "OTTO WREDE", was the personal mount of Lt P-E Sovelius, a pilot of 4/LeLv 24. The leaping puma was the group insignia, Lunkula, Finland.*

Fig. 10 *The B-239s (F2A-1s) that were sold to Finland were shipped in crates to Trollhätten, Sweden, where they were assembled. Note the lack of camouflage and light blue swastikas.*

Fig. 12 *A close up of the moose insignia of 2/LeLv 24.*

Fig. 11 *BW-354, flown by Sgt H Lampi, stands out against the snow, February 1942. Note the five victory markings actually head-on silhouettes of the actual types shot down.*

Fig. 13 *The colourful pre-war markings did not last long after the service introduction of the Buffalo, but they were beautiful while they lasted. VF-2's 2-F-7 (BuNo 01412) is third section leader, hence the blue cowling and band. The tail is lemon yellow.* (USN via Hal Andrews)

Fig. 14 *Landing gear failures were endemic with the Buffalo. This F2A-2 suffered a scraped belly and bent prop as a result of just such an accident. The cause was the thin, jointed extension strut which failed with regularity. Note the ventral window.* (USN via Jim Maas)

Fig. 15 *Those F2A-2s that survived ended up as trainers. Here, BuNo 01413 is righted after a ground loop, a common experience with novice pilots, 14 July 1942.* (Jim Maas)

Fig. 16, Below *A few of the B-339Bs intended for Belgium were delivered to RCAF bases after the fall of the Low Countries, still in Belgian markings. They were taken over by the RAF and earmarked for FAA units in the Mid-East.* (RCAF via Hal Andrews)

Almost all the remaining export Buffaloes were B-339s, essentially de-navalized F2A-2s, except that all were completed with wing armament. In fact, many were delivered before the Navy's examples from the same assembly line. The Belgians put in the first order, for B-339Bs, powered by the export R-1820-G105A. Forty were ordered and completed between April and July 1940. Of these, two had arrived, crated, at Bordeaux-Merignac in June, where they were captured by the Germans. Another batch was en route to Bordeaux on the French carrier *Bearn* when France was overrun. *Bearn* turned around and made for Martinique where the Belgian Buffaloes were off-loaded. There they appear to have rotted away, the victims of neglect. The rest of the Belgian Buffaloes were added to the British order for delivery to the FAA. These were shipped to the Mid-East, most eventually ending up on Crete.

Fig. 17 *XF2A-2 cockpit layout − port side.*

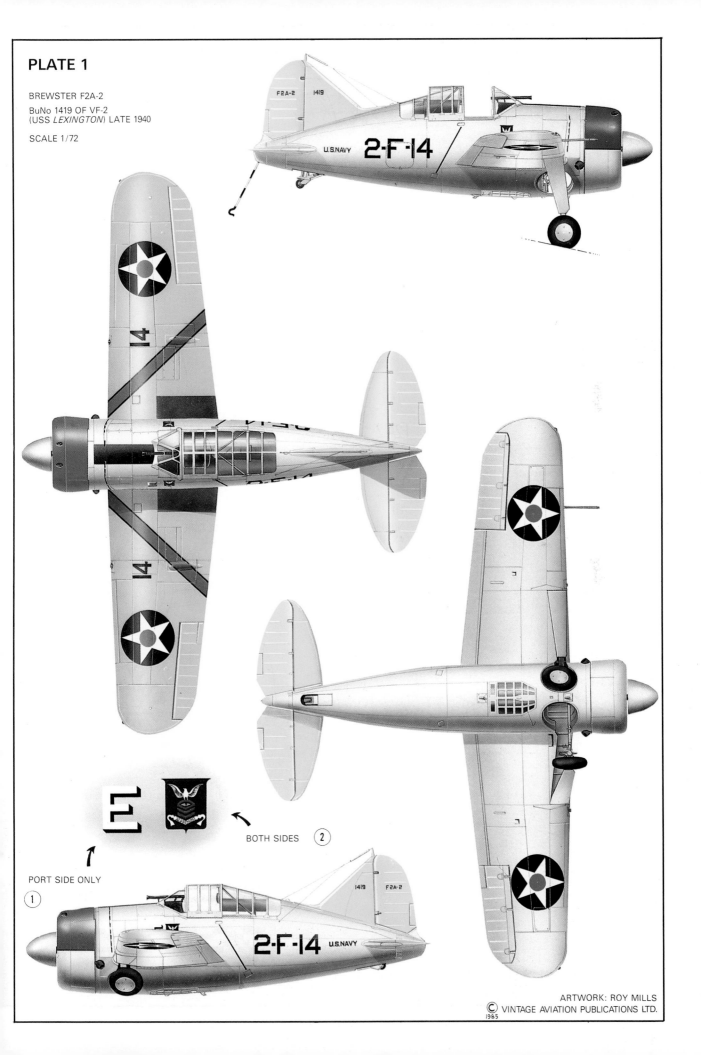

PLATE 1

BREWSTER F2A-2
BuNo 1419 OF VF-2
(USS *LEXINGTON*) LATE 1940

SCALE 1/72

PORT SIDE ONLY

BOTH SIDES

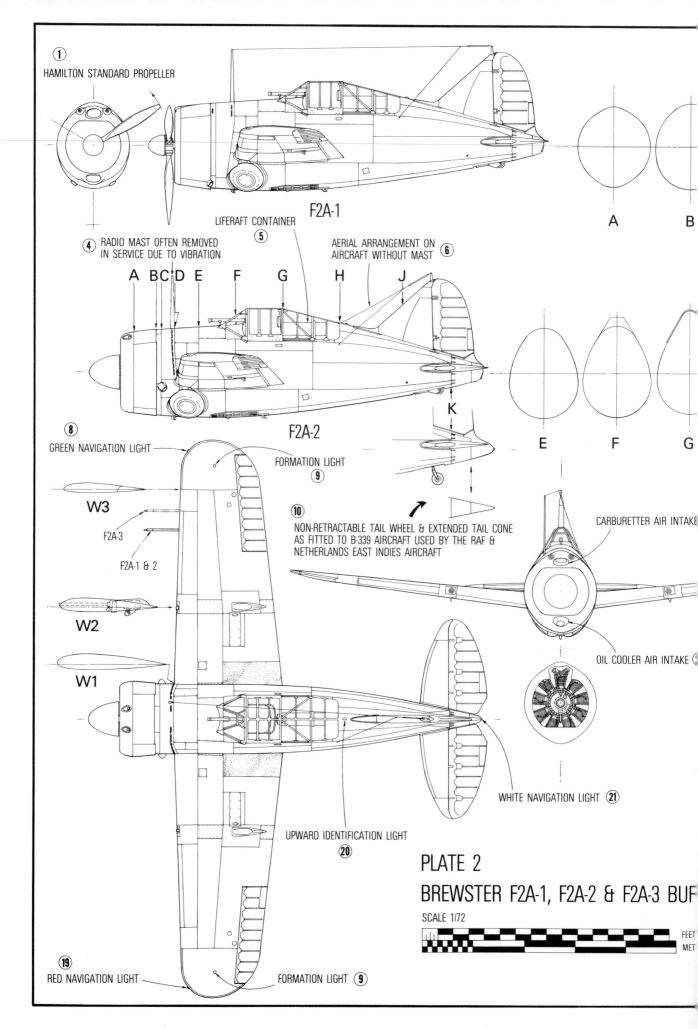

① HAMILTON STANDARD PROPELLER

F2A-1

A   B

LIFERAFT CONTAINER
⑤

④ RADIO MAST OFTEN REMOVED
IN SERVICE DUE TO VIBRATION

AERIAL ARRANGEMENT ON
AIRCRAFT WITHOUT MAST ⑥

A BC D E   F   G   H   J

F2A-2

K

E   F   G

⑧
GREEN NAVIGATION LIGHT

FORMATION LIGHT
⑨

W3

F2A-3

F2A-1 & 2

W2

W1

⑩
NON-RETRACTABLE TAIL WHEEL & EXTENDED TAIL CONE
AS FITTED TO B-339 AIRCRAFT USED BY THE RAF &
NETHERLANDS EAST INDIES AIRCRAFT

CARBURETTER AIR INTAKE

OIL COOLER AIR INTAKE

WHITE NAVIGATION LIGHT ㉑

UPWARD IDENTIFICATION LIGHT
⑳

PLATE 2

BREWSTER F2A-1, F2A-2 & F2A-3 BUF

SCALE 1/72

FEET
MET

⑲
RED NAVIGATION LIGHT

FORMATION LIGHT ⑨

10

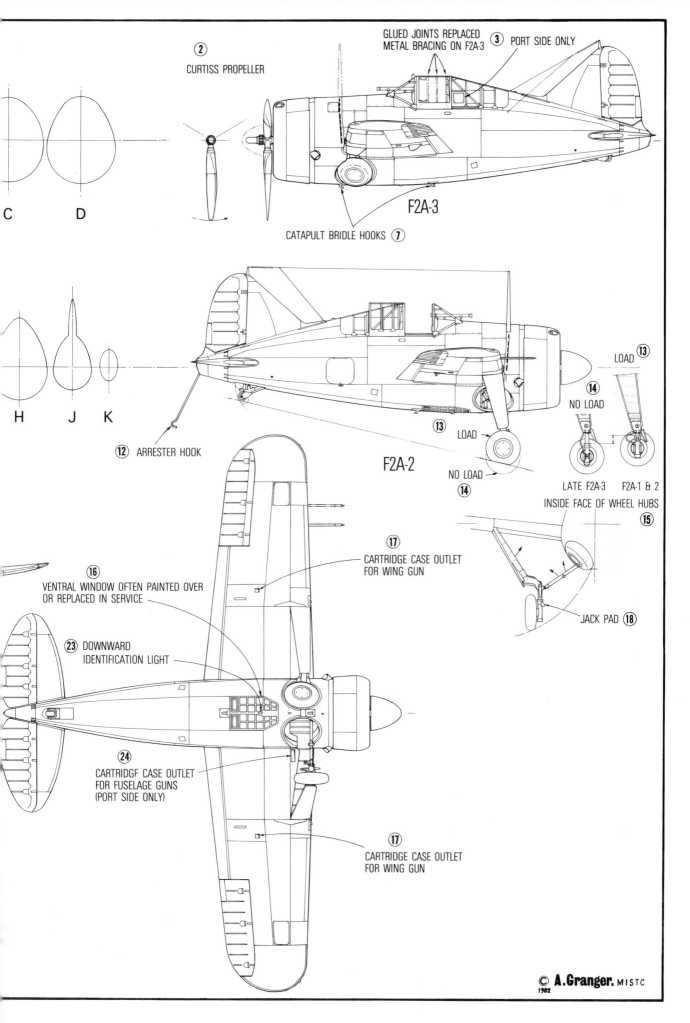

② CURTISS PROPELLER

C   D

GLUED JOINTS REPLACED
METAL BRACING ON F2A-3   ③ PORT SIDE ONLY

F2A-3

CATAPULT BRIDLE HOOKS ⑦

H   J   K

⑫ ARRESTER HOOK

F2A-2

LOAD ⑬

⑭ NO LOAD

⑬ LOAD

NO LOAD

⑭

LATE F2A-3   F2A-1 & 2
INSIDE FACE OF WHEEL HUBS
⑮

CARTRIDGE CASE OUTLET
FOR WING GUN ⑰

⑯ VENTRAL WINDOW OFTEN PAINTED OVER
OR REPLACED IN SERVICE

㉓ DOWNWARD
IDENTIFICATION LIGHT

JACK PAD ⑱

㉔ CARTRIDGF CASE OUTLET
FOR FUSELAGE GUNS
(PORT SIDE ONLY)

⑰ CARTRIDGE CASE OUTLET
FOR WING GUN

© A.Granger. MISTC
1982

11

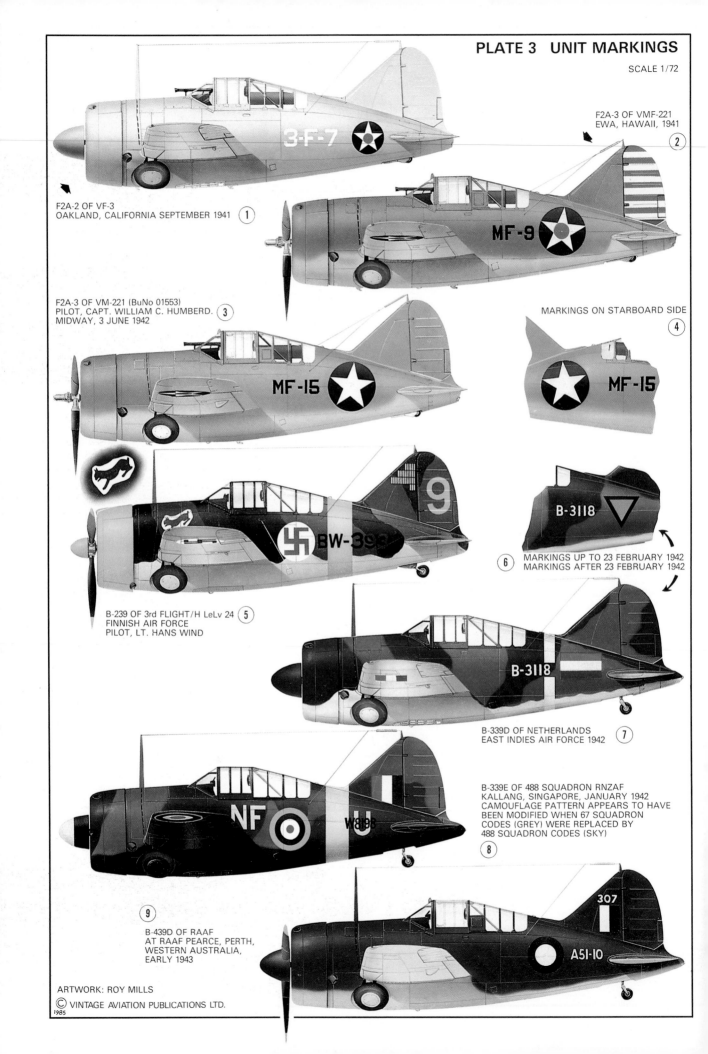

PLATE 3 UNIT MARKINGS

SCALE 1/72

F2A-3 OF VMF-221
EWA, HAWAII, 1941 (2)

3-F-7

MF-9

F2A-2 OF VF-3
OAKLAND, CALIFORNIA SEPTEMBER 1941 (1)

F2A-3 OF VM-221 (BuNo 01553)
PILOT, CAPT. WILLIAM C. HUMBERD. (3)
MIDWAY, 3 JUNE 1942

MARKINGS ON STARBOARD SIDE (4)

MF-15

MF-15

BW-393

B-3118

(6) MARKINGS UP TO 23 FEBRUARY 1942
MARKINGS AFTER 23 FEBRUARY 1942

B-239 OF 3rd FLIGHT/H LeLv 24 (5)
FINNISH AIR FORCE
PILOT, LT. HANS WIND

B-3118

B-339D OF NETHERLANDS (7)
EAST INDIES AIR FORCE 1942

NF W8198

B-339E OF 488 SQUADRON RNZAF
KALLANG, SINGAPORE, JANUARY 1942
CAMOUFLAGE PATTERN APPEARS TO HAVE
BEEN MODIFIED WHEN 67 SQUADRON
CODES (GREY) WERE REPLACED BY
488 SQUADRON CODES (SKY)
(8)

(9)

B-439D OF RAAF
AT RAAF PEARCE, PERTH,
WESTERN AUSTRALIA,
EARLY 1943

307

A51-10

ARTWORK: ROY MILLS

© VINTAGE AVIATION PUBLICATIONS LTD.

1985

Fig. 18 *XF2A-2 cockpit layout – starboard side.*

13

One of the British-impressed Belgian Buffaloes, RAF s/n AS426, was tested at RAE Farnborough and found unsuitable to operate as a land-based fighter over Europe. (Not surprising, considering the age and origins of the design!) The decision was made to ship the 170 RAF-ordered B-339E Buffalo Is (s/ns W8131-8250 & AN168-217) to the Far East, where the threat posed by the Japanese was seen as being of much lower quality. Delivery of these to Singapore began in December 1940. Seventy-two B-339Ds for the Dutch East Indies Air Force (s/ns B-395-3166) differing only in having .30 calibre machine guns in the wings, began to arrive in mid-1941. The Dutch also ordered 20 B-439Ds (essentially F2A-3s, s/ns B-3167-3186) with 1200hp R-1820-G205A Cyclones. Seventeen of these ended up being impressed into the RAAF as A-51-1-17. At least two of these ended up in USAAF colours with the 5th AF in Australia.

These assorted B-339s were formed into eight squadrons flying Buffaloes in the Far East. On 8 December 1941, they were:

1-V1.G V (NEIAF)	Borneo
2-V1.G V (NEIAF)	Java
3-V1.G V (NEIAF)	Ambon
21 Sqn RAAF	Sungei Patani, Malaya
67 Sqn RAF	Mingaladon, Burma
243 Sqn RAF	Singapore with detachment at Kota Bharu, Malaya
453 Sqn RAAF	Singapore
488 Sqn RNZAF	Singapore

Many of these aircraft were of marginal serviceability due to serious lack of trained mechanics. Typical was the case of 453 Sqn which was sent without groundcrew to Ipoh, Malaya, to join the retiring 21 Squadron. That unit's mechanics were forced to try to keep two squadrons flying, with predictable results. Often considerably less than half of a squadron's aircraft were flyable and those often had degraded performance. (Valve problems with the export Cyclones were chronic.)

Unfortunately, it was in this sad shape that the allied air forces had to meet the Japanese onslaught, ready or not. Despite years of increasing tension, months of reconnaissance overflights (the very reason why a detachment of 243 Squadron was sent to Kota Bharu) and full knowledge that a Japanese military convoy was near the Kra Isthmus, several hours after enemy troops began to land, 21 Squadron's 12 Buffaloes were caught on the ground. By the end of 8 December (the same day as the attack on Pearl Harbor across the Date Line), 21 Squadron was down to four aircraft. When they withdrew to Ipoh on the 9th, one Buffalo was in combat condition.

There followed a four-day lull in the action. 453 and 488 Squadrons were given the job of protecting the sortie of *Repulse* and *Prince of Wales* but instituted no standing patrols over the warships. By the time they could respond to *Prince of Wales'* cries for help, they arrived in time to protect the escort picking up survivors. On the 13th, 453 Squadron was dispatched to Ipoh to bolster 21 Squadron. Flt Lt Vigors, a Battle of Britain veteran, proved on that same day that the Buffalo could be at the least an adequate fighter by bringing down three of the nine Japanese fighters bagged by No 453 that day, before he was himself shot down. But the next day, three Vals shot down two and damaged a third out of a flight of four Buffaloes that attacked them. By the evening of the 14th, the two squadrons had three serviceable aircraft between them. Ten more Buffaloes arrived on the 15th, while 2-V1.G V arrived at Singapore from Java.

The action continued at the same pace, with the same dreary results. On the 19th, two more Buffaloes were destroyed on the ground at Ipoh, the five that could still fight were withdrawn under 453 Squadron to Kuala Lumpur. Ten fresh Buffaloes arrived that evening but six were lost in combat the next day and one more on the 21st. 453 Squadron retreated to Singapore on 22 December with eight Buffaloes, the last allied aircraft to leave Malaya.

Fig. 19 *The first B-339E Buffalo I (s/n W8131) is seen in US civil registry just before being turned over to the RAF.* (Hal Andrews)

On the 21st, 67 Squadron at Mingaladon was engaged for the first time, in company with the P-40s of the 3rd Squadron of the AVG, against Japanese Army Ki 27 Nates. The Buffaloes did reasonably well against this even-more obsolescent opposition, bringing down two enemies, on the average, for each Buffalo lost. There was a small reserve of aircraft but no back-up supply of pilots. The expected attrition caused a gradual lowering of the squadron's strength, until, in March 1942, it effectively ceased to exist.

Figs. 20 & 21 *AS430 was one of the ex-Belgian B-339Bs taken over by the RAF in May 1940. The colours are "Battle of Britain" standard with large fin flash characteristic of mid-1940.* (RCAF via Hal Andrews)

The two Dutch squadrons which had remained in the Indies also saw their first action near the end of December. Tarakan, Borneo, where a detachment of 1-V1.G V was based, was raided on the 26th, two Buffaloes being lost. A Japanese raid on Ambon on 13 January cost 3-V1.G V another pair. On the 20th, the five B-339Ds that remained of 2-V1.G V at Singapore were dispatched to bolster 1-V1.G V on Borneo. Flying out of Samarinda, the combined force accounted for four Japanese raiders in the next week, but lost five of their own. At the end of January, they withdrew to Java. Losses accelerated after their transfer. On 9 February, eight Buffaloes of 3-V1.G V were shot down, the remnants of that unit being absorbed by 2-V1.G V. On the 19th, a fighter sweep by A6M2s of the Japanese Navy's Tainan AC brought down six Buffaloes for the loss of one Zero. By the 23rd of February, all remaining Dutch Brewsters, a total of seven, were withdrawn to Ngoro. Their last mission was on 5 March 1942. Java surrendered three days later, several Buffaloes falling intact into Japanese hands.

Singapore had 54 Buffaloes at the end of 1941, but incessant Japanese attacks whittled this number down rapidly. After a series of particularly heavy raids on 27 January, only the six Brewsters of 453 Squadron, along with eight Hurricanes, remained on the island. 453 Squadron had fought continually from the beginning of the campaign to its bloody end, claiming at least 34 enemy aircraft. Now, at the beginning of February 1942, it joined the general exodus and flew off to Java en route to Australia.

A number of reasons can be cited to explain the very different outcome of this aerial campaign as opposed to that fought by the Finns, but quality of opposing aircraft cannot be considered a major factor. RAF and Dutch Buffaloes fell not only to newer Zeros and Oscars, but also to decidedly inferior Nates and Claudes. The Finns flew the Buffalo with continued success against aircraft that could outfly it by a considerable margin. The explanation for the Brewster's failure in the Pacific has to be found elsewhere. Some of the reasons can be found in the difference between the Buffaloes flown on the two fronts. The Finnish B-239s were slower but considerably more responsive than the B-339s. The earlier mark might have fared better against the Japanese. The poor quality of maintenance in the Far East, and the consequent lowered performance of the Buffaloes that fought there, must also be considered part of the cause. Part must also be blamed on pilot quality. While the Japanese pilots were survivors of a rigorous training system, and many were seasoned veterans of the 'China Incident', the CO of 453 Squadron had cause to complain on several occasions of the inadequate preparation of his fliers. The RAF had originally sent its Buffaloes to the Far East because of a serious underestimation of the quality of both Japanese aircraft and pilots. This same misjudgement led to the posting to Malaya of squadrons composed largely of undertrained Australians and New Zealanders with a very thin leavening of veterans. The Buffalo lost in the Far East as much because it was outflown, as for any other reason.

Fig. 22, Above *B-3119, one of the Dutch B-339Ds, is seen over the US. Again, notice the US civil registry on the rudder and wing, which would be removed before delivery. Note also the repetition of the serial number on the wing leading edge.* (USN via Tailhook Assn.)

Fig. 23, Right *The last B-439D, s/n B3-186, is seen during its final painting process. As with most of these Dutch F2A-3s, it eventually ended up in RAAF hands.* (USN-NARS)

The Marines of VMF-221 had a somewhat better excuse for their poor showing. They were flying the last production model of the Buffalo, the F2A-3 (Model B-439). This variant differed from the last batch of F2A-2s only in having the R-1820-40 moved forward by nine inches. The reason for this change was to correct centre of gravity problems that had cropped up in the 'dash-2' with the introduction of the heavier engine, the extra room forward of the canopy being used for increased fuel stowage. As a result, loaded weight continued to escalate. The F2A-3 was 1,500lb (680kg) heavier than the prototype. Top speed dropped by 3mph (4.8km/h) to 321mph (517km/h), and the climb rate continued to suffer. The increased weight also put more strain on the already weak landing gear, which continued to fail at an alarming rate. The cumulative effect of the increasing weight resulted in excessive wing loading in the F2A-3, further degrading manoeuvrability. Despite the general opinion that the 'dash-3' was less of an aircraft than the 'dash-2', the US Navy ordered 108 (BuNos 01516-01623).

Four US Navy squadrons (VF-2, -3, -9 & VS-201) received the F2A-3. VF-2 traded in its F2A-2s for 'dash-3's in September 1941. VF-3 began the transition but never finished as it traded all its Buffaloes for Wildcats just before Pearl Harbor. VF-9 likewise never completed transition into the Buffalo. VF-2 kept its Buffaloes until late January 1942, when it, too, received F4F-3s. During its two months of war, the total of action seen by VF-2s Buffaloes was firing on a suspected submarine contact on 10 January. Raids on Jaluit, Makin and Wake were successively planned and cancelled. VS-201, which had seven F2A-3s along with 13 SOCs, passed on its Buffaloes not long after VF-2.

Fig. 24, Above *The bow of* **Lexington** *is full of 18 F2A-3s of VMF-221 as she leaves San Diego on 14 October 1941. They were off-loaded at Pearl Harbor and based at MCAS Ewa until they were committed to the defence of Wake in mid-December.* (USN-NARS)

Fig. 25, Below *No Marine Buffaloes were assigned carrier duty, but all Marine squadrons had to be carrier qualified. The Buffalo was stable at landing speeds and was easy to fly on and off carriers, but continued to be plagued by landing-gear failures. This F2A-3 ended up in the catwalk because the left gear collapsed.*

(USN via Jim Mass)

Fig. 26 *Another landing-gear failure, another training accident, BuNo 01607, F2A-3, 26 April 1942.* (Jim Maas)

Fig. 27 *Before the fiasco of the attempted relief of Wake, VMF-221's Buffaloes spent a brief interlude at Ewa, Hawaii, during November 1941. They left Pearl Harbor on Saratoga on 16 December, but turned back from Wake on the 23rd. They were flown off to Sand Island, Midway, on Christmas Day.* (USMC via Tailhook Assn.)

Fig. 28 *BuNo 01573, an F2A-3 of VMF-221, lies derelict at the edge of the apron. The colours are early-war blue grey and light grey with red and white rudder stripes. The markings are "MF-8" in black.*
(Jim Maas)

VMF-221 was one of four Marine squadrons to fly the Buffalo but was the only one to see action. (The other three squadrons were VMF-111, -211 & -222.) The sad fate of VMF-221 has already been described. Thirteen of 19 Buffaloes were shot down, but the results were hardly one-sided. While exact figures will probably never be known, at least 20 Japanese aircraft were claimed by VMF-221 that morning. Even the 'dash-3' Buffalo could hold its own against a Zero if well flown, but the limits of the design had obviously been exceeded.

Any other Buffaloes left in Navy or Marine inventory were rapidly turned over to training units. Even in this role it didn't last long, as it was hardly a forgiving mount for novice pilots. Nearly all had disappeared by the end of 1943, though some flew as late as 1945. A single F2A-3 airframe received a pressurized cockpit and was dubbed the XF2A-4, but the Navy wanted nothing further to do with the Buffalo. The only preserved examples of the Brewster Buffalo, fittingly, are in Finland, the only place where the tubby little fighter was appreciated.

Fig. 29 & 30 *Lt Cdr J C Clifton led his training unit out of NAS Pensacola. The wingtips and rudder were light grey, presumably replacements off a hangar queen that was never repainted. Training aircraft were rarely pretty.* (USN-NARS)

SPECIFICATIONS

XF2A-1:

Dimensions: length, 25ft 6in (7773mm); height, 11ft 9in (3582mm); span, 35ft 0in (10668mm); wing area, 208.9 sq ft (19.408sq m).

Weights: loaded weight, 4,832lb (2192kg).

Performance: max speed at 15,200ft (4328m), 280mph (451km/h); cruising speed, 180mph (290km/h); ceiling, 29,800ft (9083m); range, 650miles (1046km).

Powerplant: Wright XR-1820-22 Cyclone of 850hp take-off power.

Armament: 1 × .30 calibre machine gun; 1 × .50 calibre machine gun.

F2A-1:

Dimensions: length, 26ft 0in (7925mm); height, 11ft 11in (3632mm); span, 35ft 0in (10668mm); wing area, 208.9sq ft (19.408sq m).

Weights: loaded weight, 5,040lb (2286kg); empty weight, 3,785lb (1717kg).

Performance: max speed at 17,000ft (5182m), 301mph (484km/h); cruising speed, 160mph (258km/h); rate of climb, 3,060ft/min (993m/min); ceiling, 32,500ft (9905m); range, 1,095miles (1762km).

Powerplant: Wright R-1820-34 Cyclone of 950hp take-off power.

Armament: 1 × .30 calibre machine gun; 1 or 3 × .50 calibre machine guns.

F2A-2:

Dimensions: length, 25ft 7in (7797mm); height, 12ft 0in (3658mm); span, 35ft 0in (10668mm); wing area, 208.9 sq ft (19.408sq m).

Weights: loaded weight, 5,945lb (2697kg); empty weight, 4,576lb (2076kg).

Performance: max speed at 16,500ft (5029m), 324mph (521km/h); cruising speed, 157mph (253km/h); rate of climb, 2,500ft/min (762m/min); ceiling, 34,000ft (10363m); range, 1,015miles (1634km).

Powerplant: Wright R-1820-40 Cyclone of 1,200hp take-off power.

Armament: 4 × .50 calibre machine guns.

F2A-3:

Dimensions: length, 26ft 4in (8026 mm); height, 12ft 0in (3658mm); span, 35ft 0in (10668mm); wing area, 208.9sq ft (19.408sq m).

Weights: loaded weight, 6,321lb (2867kg); empty weight, 4,732lb (2146kg).

Performance: max speed at 13,500ft (4114m), 321mph (517km/h); cruising speed, 160mph (258km/h); rate of climb, 2,290ft/min (6733m/min); ceiling, 30,000ft (9144m); range, 965miles (1553km).

Powerplant: Wright R-1820-40 Cyclone of 1,200hp take-off power.

Armament: 4 × .50 calibre machine guns.

GRUMMAN F4F WILDCAT

SNJ & SNV
Flight Instructor
Rusty Lunning
Sanford Fla - 1945
USN R-Rocky Phillips Inst

21

Fig. 2 *The XF4F-2 bears surprisingly little resemblance to the production Wildcat. Most of the external shapes were progressively changed, but the basic structure is there. This is the aircraft that 'flew-off' against the Brewster Buffalo and lost.* (Grumman)

Designed to the same 1935 requirement as the much maligned Brewster Buffalo, the Grumman F4F Wildcat seemed to live in the shadow of the Brewster for much of its early career. Indeed, the first Wildcat was ordered only as a back-up, in case the Buffalo failed. Rejecting the understudy role, Grumman's 'Iron Works' redesigned the F4F into a pugnacious little mid-wing fighter that easily outperformed the early Buffalo but suffered from even more nagging development problems than the F2A, leading to the Buffalo being preferred over the Wildcat on several occasions. Because of these problems, both aircraft suffered an overlong gestation period, with the result that in combat they often found themselves facing newer, superior opponents. Yet, while the Brewster Buffalo rapidly faded from the scene after demonstrating its inability to survive Pacific combat, the Wildcat was fated to serve on in vast numbers, in front line service, to war's end.

The differences between the two aircraft, the reasons why the Buffalo's production run was less than 500 while almost 8,000 Wildcats were built, are difficult to find in a specifications table. In terms of statistics, there was often little to choose from between the early production aircraft, though the Wildcat tended to have a slight edge in top speed. Despite the persistent delays, the US Navy seemed to have an underlying preference for the Wildcat and faith in Grumman and its ability to iron out the Wildcat's problems. That faith was more than borne out. The Wildcat did indeed emerge as a tough, workmanlike machine, destined to far outshine the Buffalo in the eyes of history. While neither fighter will ever be thought of as great, though both had their moments of glory, there was one important difference between the two that justifies the USN's preference for the Grumman design. While every design change to the Buffalo seemed to reduce manoeuvrability and worsen overall performance, every change to the Wildcat seemed to make it better (or at least not significantly worse). A good, stable aircraft from the outset, the Wildcat remained docile and easy to fly to its last catapult launch by the last 'green' pilot off the last escort carrier. The Wildcat's feats in 'holding the line' in the early days of the war, until better fighters could come along, are well known. It is a mark of the basic quality of the design that it was in those last days, when by any normal standard it should have long since been retired, that the first of the 'cats was once again 'holding the line' in one of the most dramatic battles of the war.

From the beginning, the F4F was unique. No other major production World War 2 – vintage monoplane fighter started out life as a biplane! With a history of producing handy biplane fighters for the Navy (FF-1 'Fifi', F2F & F3F which first flew in 1935), Grumman instinctively turned again to the biplane concept when the USN requested a new fighter in 1935. The day of the biplane was over, however, and even the hidebound conservatives of BuAer knew it. Even though Grumman was awarded a contract for a single XF4F-1, the USN made clear its preference for the Brewster's monoplane design. Finally spurred to action, Grumman informed BuAer that it would produce a prototype to a revised, monoplane configuration within the allotted time span. In fact, the XF4F-2 flew for the first time on 2 September 1937, a full two months before the first Buffalo.

What emerged from the Bethpage plant was obviously a Grumman, the family resemblance to the preceding biplanes being considerable. Except for raising the single wing up to the fuselage mid-line and moving the cockpit forward to counterbalance the loss of an upper wing, the XF4F-2 looked very much like an F3F.

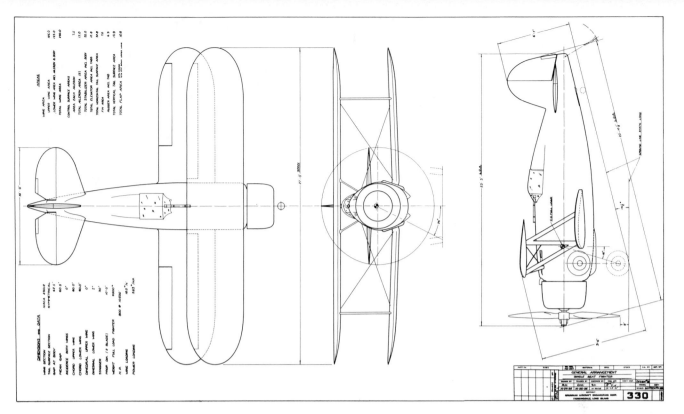

Fig. 3 *As far as the XF4F-1 ever got, a set of blueprints. It would have been a clean, but otherwise conventional, biplane.* (Grumman)

The most distinctive of Grumman characteristics, the stubby, deep-bellied fuselage, was retained, because the XF4F's landing gear was identical to that of all the earlier Grummans'. Grumman started its corporate life as a subcontractor to Loening, making the short, double-strutted retracting landing gear that was one of the revolutionary features of the Loening amphibians. When Leroy Grumman set off on his own in 1929, he took with him the right to incorporate the still novel retracting landing gear in his designs. It was the inclusion of landing gear retraction that helped sell the USN on the FF-1 in 1931. The short stroke of the Loening landing gear, which only had to be long enough to give ground clearance to an amphibian's float, required the deep-belly that became a hallmark of early Grumman designs. The landing gear employed in the XF4F was simple and proven, suffering only from a too narrow track, again a result of its amphibian origins.

Fig. 4 *In the middle of its metamorphosis, the XF4F-3 looks much more like a Wildcat, with the lengthened nose and squared-off extremities. Only the tail needs to be added. The prototype still had cowling guns, which disappeared on production aircraft.* (Grumman)

Fig. 5 *The first F4F-3s arrived in time for the last pre-war manoeuvres. The giant Louisiana wargames of autumn 1941 involved these USN fighters on the Red side, hence the red crosses in six positions.* (USN-NARS)

The XF4F-2 was of entirely conventional construction. The airframe was all-metal with stressed aluminium skin except for fabric-covered control surfaces. The rounded wing employed a NACA 230-series airfoil which gave excellent handling. Armament was a pair of .50 (12.7mm) machine guns in the tapering cowling. The prototype's engine, a Pratt & Whitney R-1830-66 Twin Wasp, was a major source of trouble. The Twin Wasp was a 14-cylinder, twin-row radial of 1,050hp takeoff power. It featured a single-stage, single-speed supercharger that helped deliver 900hp at 12,000ft (3658m). There was nothing novel about the Twin Wasp in this configuration, yet from the start, the new version suffered a series of problems that would handicap the XF4F-2. In particular, recurrent main bearing failures grounded the prototype time and again. While these problems were eventually ironed out, it was too late to help the XF4F in its first round of tests.

Despite intimations of engine troubles, the XF4F-2 entered a fly-off against its two competitors for the US Navy contract (the XF2A-1 and the Seversky XNF-1 – a navalized P-35) in early 1938. When the Twin Wasp was working, the Grumman was clearly faster than its competition. It had a 10mph edge over the Buffalo and was 40mph faster than the Seversky. Its handling was marginally inferior to that of the Buffalo, but it was engine problems which finally decided the issue. These culminated in a seizure while in the landing pattern on 11 April, the prototype crashing in a ploughed field. The pilot was uninjured and the damage to the airframe was minor (it was flying again in two weeks), but the effect on the selection committee was more serious. They recommended the Buffalo over the XF4F-2, the former receiving a production contract in June 1938.

This should have ended the story, but, fortunately for the US Navy, it did not. Everyone at Grumman, and few stubborn souls at BuAer, believed that the XF4F was basically superior to the Buffalo and felt that another attempt was in order. Grumman went back to the drawing boards again, coming up with the XF4F-3, which won a prototype contract in October 1938. The 'dash-3' was in fact a dramatic attempt on the part of

Fig. 6 *With reliability problems plaguing the two-stage Twin Wasp, the Navy turned to a simpler single-stage version. The XF4F-6 (BU No 7031) served as a test bed for that installation, which went into production as the F4F-3A. (This view of the XF4F-6 is actually a fine study of the appearance of a standard F4F-3. Production F4F-3As lacked the intercooler intake above the cowling.)* (Grumman)

Fig. 7 *The first ten Martlet IIs (G-36B) were externally identical to the F4F-3A. Note the lack of intercooler air scoop. These were the first RAF F4Fs assigned to sea duty and had the distinction of claiming the Wildcat's first carrier-borne kill.* (Grumman)

Grumman to produce an aircraft that would be clearly superior to any competition. The XF4F-2's minor handling deficiencies were to be solved by increasing the span of all flying surfaces. Wing span went from 34 to 38ft (10.363 to 11.582m), area increasing from 232 to 260sq ft (21.554 to 24.155sq m). The gross weight rose from 5400 to 6000lb (2450 to 2722kg). Armament was increased by moving the two .50 (12.7mm) machine guns to wing positions and replacing them in the cowling with a pair of .30s (7.6mm). The two-position Hamilton-Standard propeller was replaced by a Curtiss-Electric constant-speed model. But the most immediately obvious external difference from the 'dash-2', from which the XF4F-3 was rebuilt (even retaining the same Bu No, 0383), was the squared tips on all flying surfaces. Less obvious was a slightly extended engine cowling, which now covered a different version of the Twin Wasp.

This was the heart of the XF4F-3, the XR-1830-76 with its two-stage, two-speed supercharger. Rated at 1,200hp for takeoff, the radial, because of its two-stage blower, was able to deliver 1,050hp at 11,000ft (3353m) and a remarkable 1000hp at 19,000ft (5791m). It represented a daring gamble on Grumman's part which eventually paid off handsomely but seemed, in the short run, to be the height of foolishness. While not new, neither were two-stage superchargers common or particularly reliable in 1938. Adding the second stage to a supercharger greatly increased its efficiency above 10,000ft (3048m), but not without paying a price. The greater complexity of the two-stage blower introduced a whole new series of problems to the Twin Wasp just as the bearing failures were being resolved. On 'high blower', the engine ran faster, and therefore hotter, at high altitude where cooling air was scarcer. Further, the air that came from the first stage compressor had to be cooled before going to the second stage or it would be so hot when it was fed into the cylinders as to cause

premature detonation ('knock'). This required adding an intercooler between the stages. A related problem was that at the higher altitudes allowed by the new supercharger, fuel tended to boil in the carburettor, causing the engine to misfire. None of these problems related to the addition of a two-stage supercharger was beyond solution, and the work done on the XF4F-3 to solve them made the installation of similarly equipped engines in the next generation of fighters a painless process, but the progress of the F4F would be slowed for two more critical years.

The aircraft that first flew on 12 February 1939 was still far from 'finished'. New stability problems plagued the prototype which was returned to the workshop to have dihedral increased by 1 degree and the rudder horn balance enlarged. When even this didn't completely solve persistent longitudinal instability, the prototype was flown to Langley, Virginia, where it was tested in

Fig. 8 *Most of VMF-211's F4F-3As were caught on the ground and destroyed before they could fire a shot in the defence of Wake Island. Colours are sea grey and light grey. Black squadron and type designators were authorised only just before Pearl Harbor. Rudders were without the red and white stripes, not applied until January 1942. The national insignia is in glossy paint, a pre-war practice.* (USMC)

25

Fig. 9 *One of VF-12's first F4F-3As prepares to launch from* **Lexington** *as that squadron switched rapidly from Buffalos in February 1942, the last of the pre-war carrier squadrons to get its Wildcats.* (USN-NARS)

NACA's full-scale wind tunnel. On NACA's recommendation, a tail fillet was added which became standard on all F4Fs. The engine problems, because they were the result of multiple causes, were solved by a number of minor 'fixes' rather than one dramatic solution. The overheating was eventually brought under control by a combination of cuffs on the propeller and flaps at the rear of the cowling. It would be nearly two years, however, before the 'ultimate' pattern of cuffs and cowl flaps was discovered. The problem of engine misfirings was solved by pressurising the fuel system and by the use of higher octane fuels. The unreliability of the supercharger, because it stemmed from a lack of experience rather than any basic fault, eventually disappeared with time.

When the US Navy finally got its hands on the XF4F-3 in March 1939, it was impressed. The top speed was 333.5mph (537km/hr) at 20,500ft (6248m), making it faster than the F2A-2 at considerably higher altitude. Landing speed was a perfectly acceptable 68mph (109km/hr). It was obvious to BuAer that the Grumman had finally come of age, and despite the fact that the engine problems were still far from being overcome, a contract for 54 F4F-3s was let in August 1939.

So confident was Grumman in the eventual success of the F4F that the first pair (Bu Nos 1844-5) were already under construction when the contract was announced. The alterations from the prototype called for in the contract were relatively minor, but because the first two were begun before contract negotiations were complete, they lacked the most important of those changes. The first two retained the prototype's armament pattern, but all successive 'dash-3's deleted the cowling guns and added a second .50 machine gun in each wing. The in-

itial production contract also called for a strengthening of the landing gear and the addition of some minimal pilot armour. In the yet unresolved struggle against engine overheating, the first F4F-3s appeared in a number of different combinations of spinners, cuffs and cowling flaps. Eventually, the spinner was deleted altogether. Grumman guaranteed the performance of the F4F-3s, including a top speed of 350mph (563km/hr) at altitude. This they were never able to meet. No production F4F was even as fast as the prototype. Standard F4F-3s could reach 331mph (533km/hr) at 21,300ft (6492m). This was, however, the only guarantee that Grumman failed to satisfy, and the US Navy gratefully accepted its first 'dash-3' in August 1940.

Even if the US Navy had failed to order F4Fs, there would have been a ready market for the stubby little fighter. The European allies had, in 1939, awoken to the fact that war was inevitable and that they were woefully ill-prepared. Each turned to the US armaments industry to fill their needs. The French were the first to get to Grumman. With two new aircraft carriers on the stocks, they needed shipboard fighters, and ordered 100 F4F-3s (as G-36As) in late 1939. Because of a short supply of Twin Wasps, the French aircraft were to be fitted with Wright R-1820-G205A Cyclones, rated at an identical 1,200hp for takeoff, but less powerful at altitude because they had only a single-stage blower. Testing of the first G-36A began in May 1940, but France fell in that same month, and the entire 100 aircraft order was taken over by the British. The first G-36A, named Martlet I, was delivered to the Fleet Air Arm on 27 July 1940, a full month before the first US Navy delivery. Despite the fact that they had been ordered by the

Fig. 10. Above *One of the persistent problems early in the war was 'friendly fire'. Trigger-happy AA gunners shot at anything in the air, more often than not their own aircraft. In an attempt to make recognition easier, the fleet ordered the enlargement of the previously rather small national insignia and its placement in all six positions. At the same time, red and white horizontal stripes were painted on the rudder. En route to Wake Island raid, mid-February 1942, one of VF-6's F4F-3s has most of its markings and canopy covered, probably to prevent recognition from the air. ('Dash-3s' and '-3As' can be distinguished from this angle only by the number of cowling flaps. F4F-3s had a single flap on each side, while the '-3As' continued around the bottom.)* (USN-NARS)

Fig. 11. Below *On the morning of the raid, 'F-8' has its wing guns serviced and armed, while a crowd watches. F4F-3s can be distinguished from folding wing 'dash-4s' by the two gun armament and the protruding blast tubes.* (USN-NARS)

Fig. 12 *Around the time of the Marcus Island raid, VF-6 shows its mix of F4F-3s and '-3As'. The insignia enlargement instruction was implemented in a rush, leading to instances of overlapping roundels. (Officially, the wing roundel was not supposed to cover the aileron.) Enterprise, early March 1942.* (USN-NARS)

French for carrier duty, the Martlet Is were never sent to sea by the Royal Navy because of their lack of wing-folding. Nevertheless, the first F4F victory was claimed by an FAA Martlet which shot down a Ju88 over Scotland on Christmas Day, 1940. Martlet Is gained their greatest fame in the least likely of locations, operating over the North African Desert with 805 Squadron.

The problems with both the reliability and supply of the R-1830-76 continued to worry BuAer, leading to the ordering of a pair of Martlet Is as possible production prototypes for a Cyclone-powered F4F for the US Navy. The third and fourth F4F-3s were thus fitted with R-1820-40s (the US version of the G205A) and test flown in the summer of 1940 as XF4F-5s. By this time, however, the supply problems with the Twin Wasps were clearing up (although the reliability remained in question), and no further Cyclone-powered F4Fs were ordered at this time. Continuing doubts about the two-stage supercharger of the R-1830-76 led in late 1940 to the ordering of one XF4F-6 with a single-stage R-1830-90, rated at 1,200hp for take-off but only 1,000hp at 12,500ft (3810m). As might be expected, altitude performance suffered with the new engine, 319mph (513km/hr) being reached at 16,100ft (49107m), but the US Navy was willing to accept the lower speed as the price for greater reliability. 65 F4F-6s, later redesignated F4F-3As, were ordered in early 1941. When they were delivered in mid-1941, the 'dash-3A's were supplied to carrier-based units, but their shipboard career was brief and all surviving examples ended up equipping Marine units.

With the gradual taming of the two-stage blower, no

additional F4F-3As were ordered by the US Navy, but 130 more were delivered to the British as Martlet IIs and IIIs. 100 Martlet IIs were ordered in 1941 as carrier fighters for the Royal Navy. The first 10 were identical to USN F4F-3As, but the remainder incorporated the wing-folding system developed by Grumman for the F4F-4. The first of the Martlet IIs was delivered in March 1941 and the last in October. The first kill for a shipborne F4F came on 20 September 1941 when a Martlett II off HMS *Audacity* shot down an Fw200 over the Atlantic. The 30 Martlet IIIs, like the Is, were not originally ordered by the British. Greece requested F4Fs in 1940, and the US Navy agreed to the lend-lease of 30 F4F-3As. Greece fell before the first of their F4Fs could be delivered, although they were in transit when that nation was overwhelmed. They ended up at Gibraltar, where they were absorbed by the RAF as land-based Martlet IIIs, serving in the Mediterranean theatre well into 1945.

A total of 578 F4F-3s and -3As had been ordered by the US Navy by the end of 1940, but by the beginning of 1941 only 22 F4F-3s had actually been accepted. These were concentrated at NAS Norfolk where VF-4 off *Ranger* and VF-7 off *Wasp* began working up the eagerly awaited fighter. Their first 'action' in US markings was in the Winter Fleet Exercises held in the Caribbean in January 1941. (This was the only time that F4Fs were to appear in the colourful pre-war markings of the US Navy. *Wasp's* F4Fs sported black tails, *Ranger's* green.) During this working up period, two serious accidents, one fatal, resulted from untimely inflation of the wing-mounted floatation bags that were intended to keep the aircraft from sinking if it had to be ditched. They were immediately removed from all F4Fs in service and deleted from all future examples.

The 38ft (11.582m) wing span of the F4F-3 caused stowage problems in early carrier trials, leading to a Contract Change in March 1940 calling for the immediate development and inclusion on the production line of a wing-folding system for the F4F. Because the Royal Navy was simultaneously expressing an interest in folding-wing F4Fs, and because RN aircraft carriers had lower hangar clearance than their US contemporaries, Grumman chose not to employ the simple expedient of folding the wings upward. Instead, they developed a surprisingly simple and robust system that rotated the wing outer sections through 90 degrees and then folded then backwards. (The same system was used with equal success on the TBF and F6F. Other US aircraft used by the RN, most notably the popular F4U, had to have their wingtips 'clipped'.) The first flight of the folding-wing XF4F-4 came on 14 April 1941. The success of the system was immediately obvious and the F4F-4 was ordered into production as soon as the necessary changes could be made on the production line. The prototype employed a hydraulic system that folded the wings automatically, but the US Navy opted to save weight and all production F4F-4s had manually-folded wings. The new wing also brought an increase in firepower. All 'dash-4's had three .50 machine guns in each wing. The first folding-wing Wildcat was delivered at the end of 1941.

One minor variant of the Wildcat was produced in small numbers during this pre-Pearl Harbor period. Sensing the need for a carrier-based, extreme-range reconnaissance aircraft, the US Navy ordered the modification on the assembly line of 100 F4F-4s into F4F-7s. The folding wing of the F4F-4 was replaced

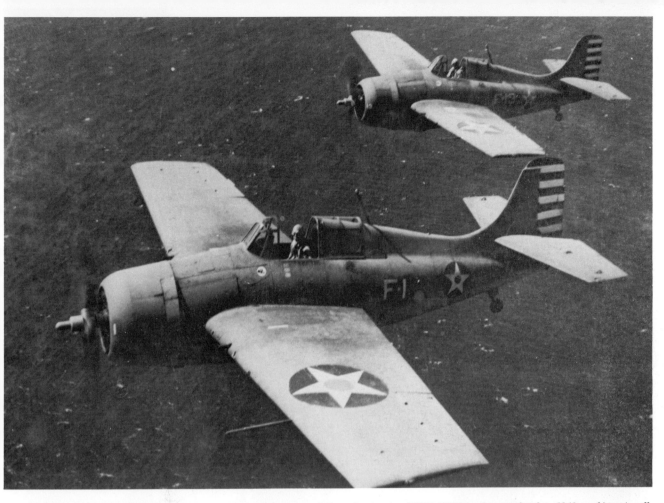

Fig. 13. Above *Each squadron interpreted the markings instructions differently. A pair of VF-3 F4F-3As show perfect late 1941 markings (small fuselage roundel), roundels in four positions only, white coding and wing numbers, except for the tail stripes. The photo can be dated to March-April 1942 by the victory markings under the cockpits. The pilots are probably the most famous pair of Wildcat 'jokes', Lt Cdr Jimmy Thach (foreground) and Lt 'Butch' O'Hare. Their victories, three and five respectively, came during the 20 February air battle off Rabaul.* (USN-NARS)

Fig. 14. Below *Markings changed too as 'factory-fresh' replacements arrived bearing current standard patterns. These VF-6 F4F-4s (note the three-gun wing) are newly arrived on Enterprise. The deckcrew lines up for sandwiches, standard lunch fare during flight ops, 18 April 1942.* (USN-NARS)

29

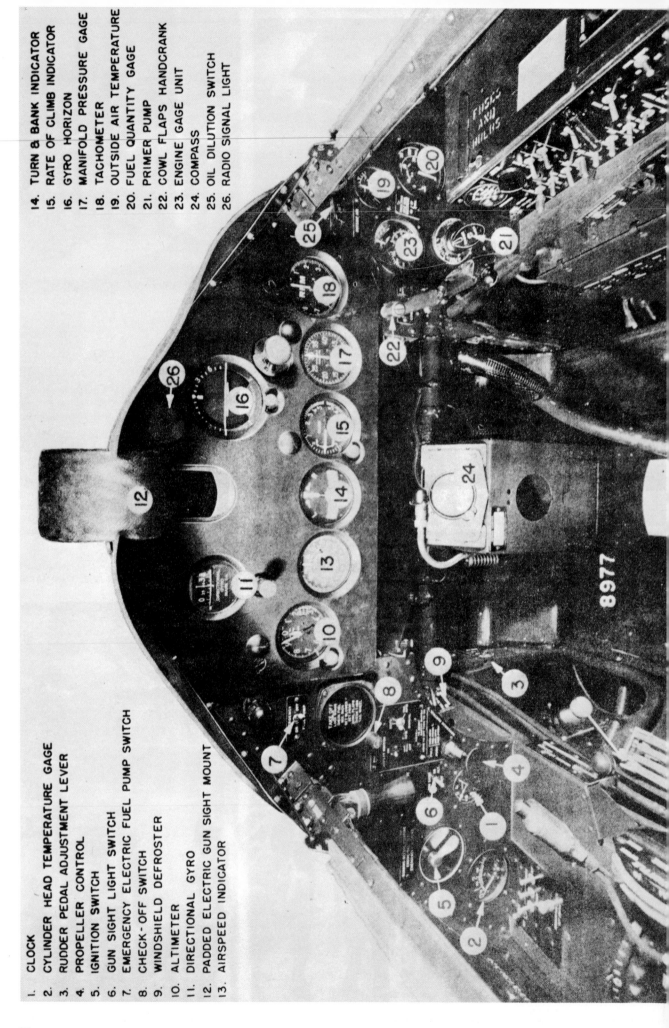

1. CLOCK
2. CYLINDER HEAD TEMPERATURE GAGE
3. RUDDER PEDAL ADJUSTMENT LEVER
4. PROPELLER CONTROL
5. IGNITION SWITCH
6. GUN SIGHT LIGHT SWITCH
7. EMERGENCY ELECTRIC FUEL PUMP SWITCH
8. CHECK-OFF SWITCH
9. WINDSHIELD DEFROSTER
10. ALTIMETER
11. DIRECTIONAL GYRO
12. PADDED ELECTRIC GUN SIGHT MOUNT
13. AIRSPEED INDICATOR

14. TURN & BANK INDICATOR
15. RATE OF CLIMB INDICATOR
16. GYRO HORIZON
17. MANIFOLD PRESSURE GAGE
18. TACHOMETER
19. OUTSIDE AIR TEMPERATURE
20. FUEL QUANTITY GAGE
21. PRIMER PUMP
22. COWL FLAPS HANDCRANK
23. ENGINE GAGE UNIT
24. COMPASS
25. OIL DILUTION SWITCH
26. RADIO SIGNAL LIGHT

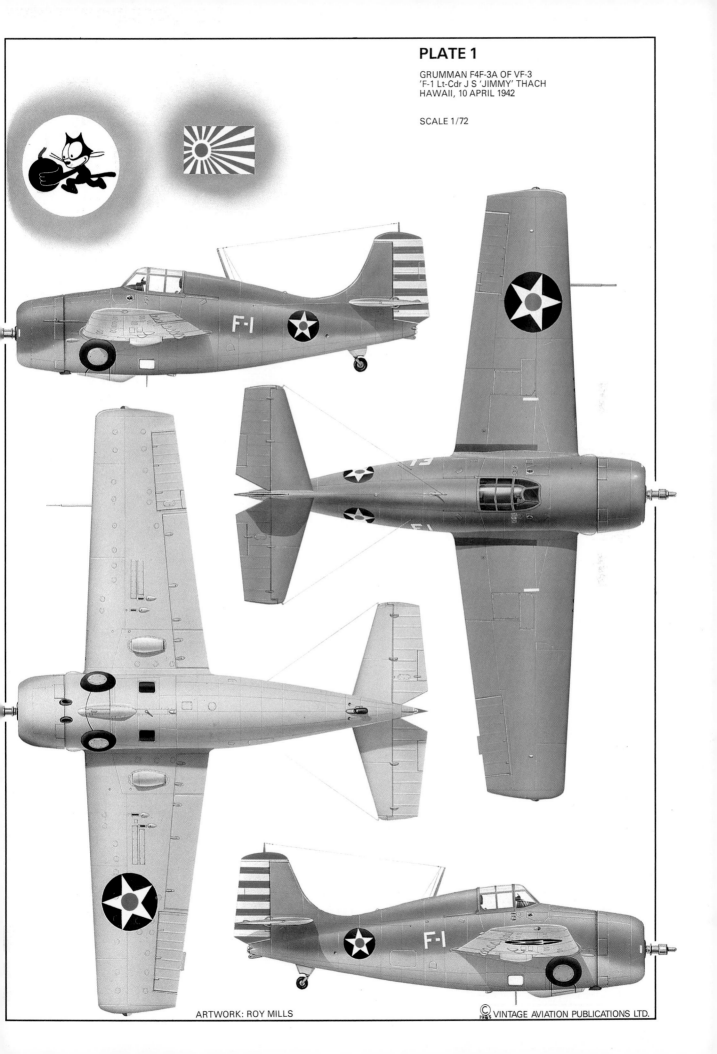

PLATE 1

GRUMMAN F4F-3A OF VF-3
'F-1 Lt-Cdr J S 'JIMMY' THACH
HAWAII, 10 APRIL 1942

SCALE 1/72

ARTWORK: ROY MILLS

© 1985 VINTAGE AVIATION PUBLICATIONS LTD.

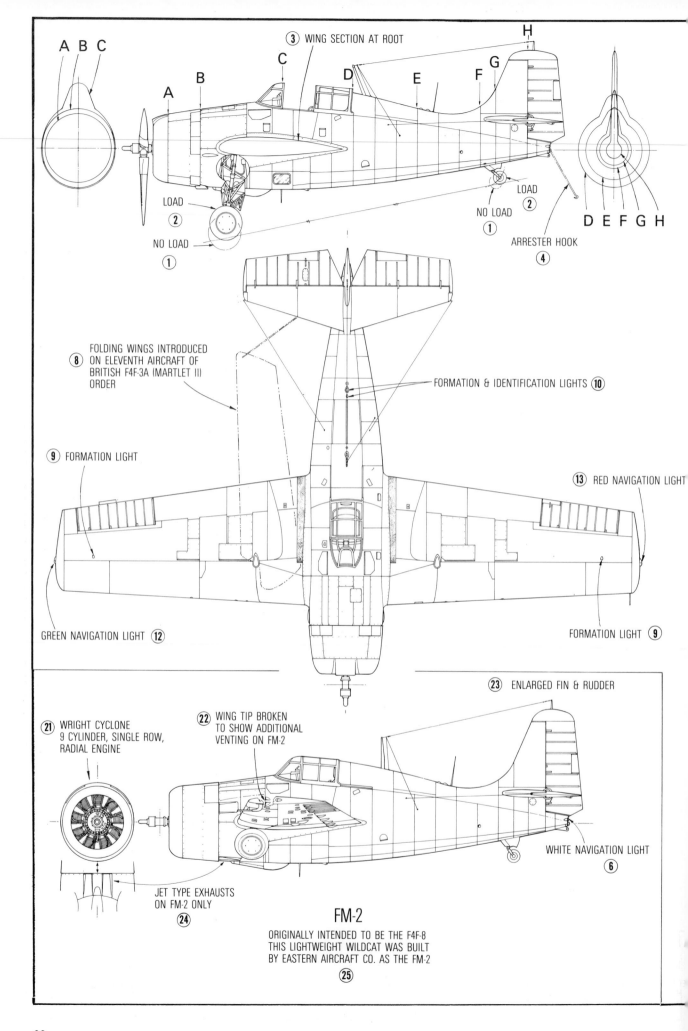

3 WING SECTION AT ROOT

A B C

A B C D E F G H

LOAD 2
NO LOAD 1

LOAD 2
NO LOAD 1

ARRESTER HOOK 4

D E F G H

8 FOLDING WINGS INTRODUCED
ON ELEVENTH AIRCRAFT OF
BRITISH F4F-3A (MARTLET II)
ORDER

FORMATION & IDENTIFICATION LIGHTS 10

9 FORMATION LIGHT

13 RED NAVIGATION LIGHT

GREEN NAVIGATION LIGHT 12

FORMATION LIGHT 9

23 ENLARGED FIN & RUDDER

21 WRIGHT CYCLONE
9 CYLINDER, SINGLE ROW,
RADIAL ENGINE

22 WING TIP BROKEN
TO SHOW ADDITIONAL
VENTING ON FM-2

WHITE NAVIGATION LIGHT
6

JET TYPE EXHAUSTS
ON FM-2 ONLY
24

FM-2

ORIGINALLY INTENDED TO BE THE F4F-8
THIS LIGHTWEIGHT WILDCAT WAS BUILT
BY EASTERN AIRCRAFT CO. AS THE FM-2
25

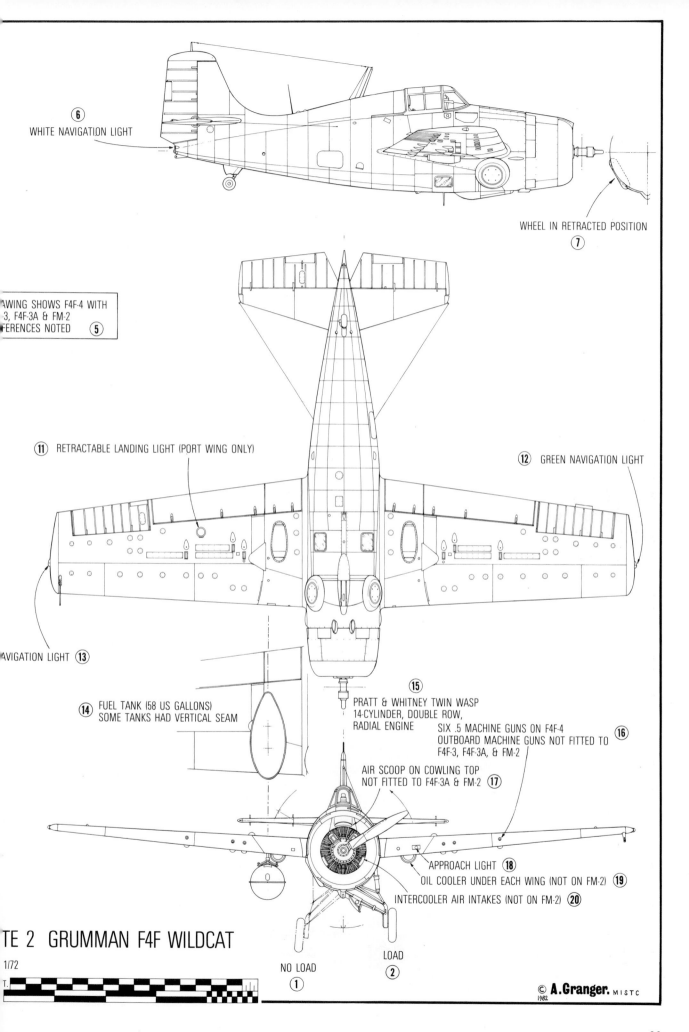

⑥ WHITE NAVIGATION LIGHT

WHEEL IN RETRACTED POSITION ⑦

⚟AWING SHOWS F4F-4 WITH
⚟-3, F4F-3A & FM-2
⚟FERENCES NOTED ⑤

⑪ RETRACTABLE LANDING LIGHT (PORT WING ONLY)

⑫ GREEN NAVIGATION LIGHT

⚟AVIGATION LIGHT ⑬

⑭ FUEL TANK (58 US GALLONS)
SOME TANKS HAD VERTICAL SEAM

⑮ PRATT & WHITNEY TWIN WASP
14-CYLINDER, DOUBLE ROW,
RADIAL ENGINE

SIX .5 MACHINE GUNS ON F4F-4
OUTBOARD MACHINE GUNS NOT FITTED TO
F4F-3, F4F-3A, & FM-2 ⑯

AIR SCOOP ON COWLING TOP
NOT FITTED TO F4F-3A & FM-2 ⑰

APPROACH LIGHT ⑱
OIL COOLER UNDER EACH WING (NOT ON FM-2) ⑲
INTERCOOLER AIR INTAKES (NOT ON FM-2) ⑳

TE 2 GRUMMAN F4F WILDCAT

1/72

NO LOAD
①

LOAD
②

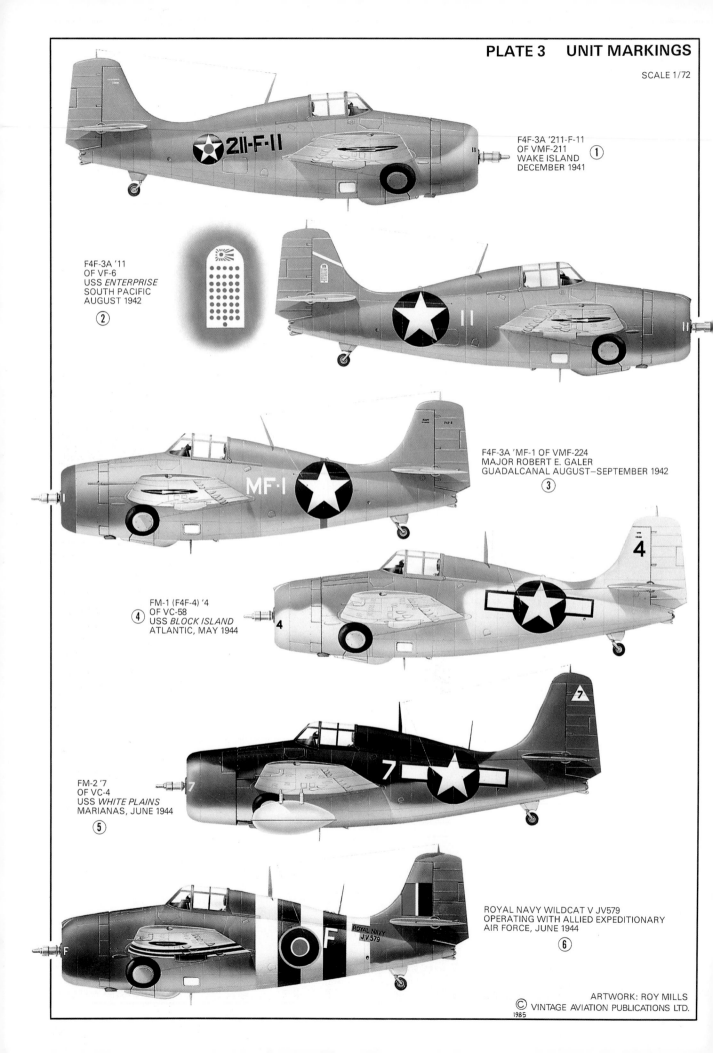

PLATE 3 UNIT MARKINGS

SCALE 1/72

F4F-3A '211-F-11
OF VMF-211
WAKE ISLAND
DECEMBER 1941
①

F4F-3A '11
OF VF-6
USS *ENTERPRISE*
SOUTH PACIFIC
AUGUST 1942
②

F4F-3A 'MF-1 OF VMF-224
MAJOR ROBERT E. GALER
GUADALCANAL AUGUST–SEPTEMBER 1942
③

FM-1 (F4F-4) '4
④ OF VC-58
USS *BLOCK ISLAND*
ATLANTIC, MAY 1944

FM-2 '7
OF VC-4
USS *WHITE PLAINS*
MARIANAS, JUNE 1944
⑤

ROYAL NAVY WILDCAT V JV579
OPERATING WITH ALLIED EXPEDITIONARY
AIR FORCE, JUNE 1944
⑥

ARTWORK: ROY MILLS
© VINTAGE AVIATION PUBLICATIONS LTD.
1985

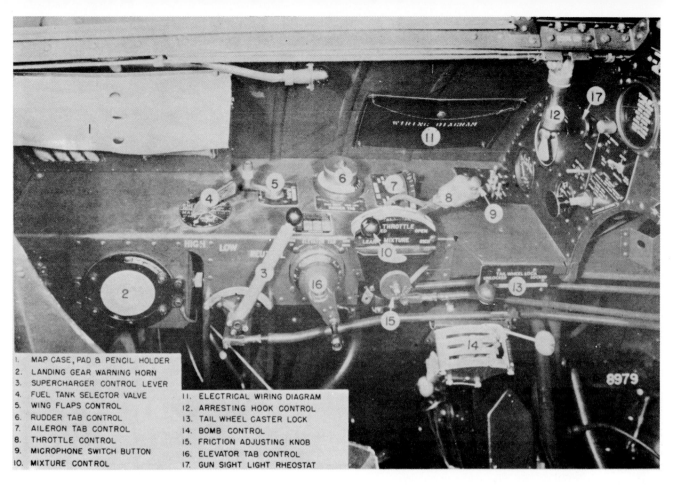

1. MAP CASE, PAD & PENCIL HOLDER
2. LANDING GEAR WARNING HORN
3. SUPERCHARGER CONTROL LEVER
4. FUEL TANK SELECTOR VALVE
5. WING FLAPS CONTROL
6. RUDDER TAB CONTROL
7. AILERON TAB CONTROL
8. THROTTLE CONTROL
9. MICROPHONE SWITCH BUTTON
10. MIXTURE CONTROL

11. ELECTRICAL WIRING DIAGRAM
12. ARRESTING HOOK CONTROL
13. TAIL WHEEL CASTER LOCK
14. BOMB CONTROL
15. FRICTION ADJUSTING KNOB
16. ELEVATOR TAB CONTROL
17. GUN SIGHT LIGHT RHEOSTAT

Fig. 16 *Cockpit – port side.* (Grumman)

Fig. 17 *Cockpit – starboard side.* (Grumman)

1. ELECTRICAL DISTRIBUTION PANEL
   & SWITCH BOX
2. FUSE PANEL - SPARE FUSES & BULBS
   UNDER DOOR
3. STARTER SWITCH
4. MICROPHONE
5. RADIO CONTROLS
6. GUN CHARGING HANDLE
7. LANDING GEAR HANDCRANK
8. HANDCRANK RATCHET RELEASE
9. LANDING GEAR POSITION INDICATOR
10. ELECTRIC CIRCUIT BREAKER RESET
    BUTTONS
11. GUN RELAY & GENERATOR CUT-OUT

Fig. 18 *Hornet prepares to leave for the war with a deck full of F4F-3s and SBC-3s, 28 February 1942. VF-8's Wildcats were landed to make room for Jimmy Doolittle's B-25s but were onboard again for Midway.* (USN-NARS)

with a restructured wing capable of holding 555 US gal (2101lt) of fuel, bringing total capacity to 685 US gal (2593lt). Despite the removal of all armour and armament, take-off weight with full fuel load rose to 10,328lb (4685kg), giving the 'dash-7' very poor performance until most of the fuel had been burned off. Nevertheless, the range and duration of the F4F-7 was nothing short of incredible. The first example flew non-stop from New York to Los Angeles in 11 hours, although the feat was never publicised because the US was now at war. In the event, only 21 F4F-7s were

actually built and only two of those, a pair at Guadalcanal, ever saw action in their intended role. Enthusiasm for the type quickly waned because the F4F-7's duration far exceeded that of any normal pilot, and it wasn't easily adaptable to any other use. Its lack of armour and armament rendered it particularly unsuited for a tactical role. Eventually all that survived were modified back to fighter configuration with normal wings.

Because the Pacific Fleet's aircraft carriers were fortuitously absent from Pearl Harbor on 7 December

Fig. 19 *Due to complaints from pilots that fleet gunners (and other fighter pilots) fired at anything red, the centre dot in the national insignia and the tail stripes were ordered to be removed just prior to Midway. Markings were by now a hodgepodge of differing patterns inconsistently applied. '7' retains the old-style large fuselage roundels, but has removed the red and displays the reduced coding (without squadron and mission designators) that the Navy was pushing for security reasons. (USN-NARS)*

1941, the Wildcats of VMF-211 on Wake Island were the first to see action in the Pacific. Having arrived only on 3 December, the Marines had just five days to become accustomed to their new home when they were attacked on the 8th (the same day as the Pearl Harbor raid on the other side of the Date Line). Warned of commencement of hostilities, the Marines had a four-plane combat air patrol (CAP) in the air at 12,000ft (3658m). Unfortunately, 36 Bettys came in at 2000ft (610m), partially masked by a cloudbank, completely unseen and unhindered. Seven of the eight Wildcats on the ground were destroyed, leaving VMF-211 with five operational fighters before it had fired a shot in anger. Instead of being discouraged, the Marines were determined to resist the inevitable invasion attempt with all of their remaining strength. When that attempt took place on the 11th, the Japanese were in for a rude surprise. One troop-carrying destroyer was sunk, a transport was damaged and two bombers were shot down, forcing the invasion force to break off and flee. But this success was not without its cost. Only two Wildcats remained in flying condition to meet the inevitable second attempt. For 11 days, the Marines dug in and prayed for reinforcements, while awaiting the return of the Japanese. (VMF-221 with a full squadron of Brewster Buffalos was enroute but arrived late.)

When the second attempt came on 22 December, it was led by 39 carrier aircraft from *Hiryu* and *Soryu*, which had been diverted from the returning Pearl Harbor Force. Two Zeros fell to one of the remaining pair of Wildcats, but both were soon shot down and the invasion continued without further aerial resistance.

Revenge became the dominant thought on American minds, retaliation for the treachery of Pearl Harbor and the humiliation of Wake and Bataan. Effective counterstrokes were desperately needed by the American public and by the fleet. But the desire to strike back at the Japanese was tempered by a great deal of caution, because the three active Pacific carriers and their squadrons represented the sum total of American offensive power. The result was a series of probing raids by the carrier groups in which the fleet's Wildcats were first bloodied.

On 1 February 1942, the US Navy began to strike back with a sortie by Rear Adm Fletcher's TF Fox (*Yorktown*) against Jaluit in the Gilberts and Vice Adml Halsey's TF How (*Enterprise*) against Roi, Wotje and Kwajalein in the Marshalls. All the targeted islands were hit, with minimal losses and damage against marginal targets. *Enterprise's* VF-6 saw its first action over Wotje, where its F4F-3As encountered Claudes, Nates and a solitary Zero. The Action Report states:

Fig. 20 *It appears that '6F13' once had a large fuselage roundel which has been overpainted. The exact date of this photo cannot be determined but it is from the time of the battle of Midway. Because of the broken tapes over the gun ports, it is obvious that this Wildcat's guns have been fired. (USN-NARS)*

Fig. 21 *Damaged in landing and already partially stripped, one of VMF-221's F4F-3As lies derelict on the apron. Sand Island, Midway. The rudder has obviously been overpainted to cover the previous tail stripes.* (USN-NARS)

The 96 (Claude) and 97 (Nate) fighters could out-manoeuvre our aircraft, including the F4Fs, and appeared faster than the SBDs. The F4Fs were much faster and had more gun power than the enemy planes, but the pilots of Fighting Squadron Six made no attempts to engage in dog fights as soon as the manoeuvrability of the enemy fighters became apparent.

Already in the Wildcat's early combat, the F4F's greatest problem came to the fore, its lack of manoeuvrability in comparison to its opposition. If Wildcat pilots tried to dogfight with the Japanese, they would lose. The best defence was instinctively obvious, simply avoiding dogfights with the enemy, using the Wildcat's superior speed and diving ability to get in and out of fights. But, while this strategy cut Wildcat losses, it also reduced its offensive effectiveness. The problem of how to get the most out of the Wildcat without dogfighting with the Japanese had no immediate solution.

The probing raids continued with TF Baker (*Lexington*) approachng Rabaul on 20 February. VF-3, was flying CAP as the task force neared launch point, when a continual series of Japanese attacks began around 11.00hr. Seven out of nine Bettys from one group were being shot down when a second raid of nine tried to sneak in from the other side. Only two Wildcats stood between this new group and *Lexington*. Fortunately, one of that pair was piloted by Lt 'Butch' O'Hare, who shot down five (or six, depending on who tells the tale) of the nine, effectively breaking up the raid and giving America one of its first genuine heros. Realising that Rabaul was well prepared to receive his attack, Vice

Fig. 22 *At the time of the battle of the Eastern Solomons.* **Enterprise's** *Wildcats carried a unique squadron victory marking. VF-6's confirmed kills to date, 41, are represented as red 'meatballs' topped by Japanese flag on a white 'tombstone', August 1942. No other US Navy squadron displayed its accumulated victories on its aircraft.* (USN-NARS)

Fig. 23 & 24 *Wildcats saw considerable service in the Atlantic, much of it rather unglamourous, but absolutely vital, anti-submarine work. The one big operation in which Wildcats starred was the Operation* **Torch** *landing in North Africa in November 1942. Here one of the VF-41's F4F-3s prepares to launch off* **Ranger**. *All USN aircraft participating in Operation* **Torch** *carried a hastily applied yellow surround to the national insignia.* (USN-NARS)

Adml Brown prudently called off the mission. Other raids were carried off against Wake on 24 February and Marcus on 4 March by *Enterprise* and against Lae and Salamaua on the north coast of New Guinea on 10 March by *Lexington* and *Yorktown*. This latter raid probably set a new record for senseless daring, as 104 aircraft were launched from the two carriers from 45nm (83km) off the south coast of the island, flew over the treacherous 13,000ft (3962m) Owen Stanley Range, attacked two minor Japanese bases and returned with the loss of only one aircraft. Such a raid, involving such

long overland distances, was not repeated by the US Navy during the war.

This brought the initial series of attacks to an end, but with a growing Japanese threat to the sea lanes between Australia and the US, *Yorktown* and *Lexington* returned shortly to the South Pacific. VF-3, however, was replaced on *Lexington* by VF-42 off *Ranger* and remained in Hawaii. VF-3, the famous 'Felix the Cat' squadron, was led by Cdr Jimmy Thach, one of the most gifted aerial tacticians of any age. Setting out to solve the problem of the Wildcat's inability to engage

Fig. 25 *29-GF-10 of* **Santee's** *VGF-29 suffered an embarrassing moment while attempting to land on 8 November 1942. The Wildcat was a tough bird and such incidents were quite rare. Aerial opposition over North Africa was slight, the Vichy French rapidly deciding that they had chosen the wrong side.* (USN-NARS)

Fig. 26 *Guadalcanal was the first chance for the Allies to win back territory in the Pacific. Marine Wildcats occupied Henderson Field as soon as it was operational and flew continual combat in the first crucial months of the struggle. In a rare moment of peace, VMF-112 and -122 Wildcats are parked in a random pattern around the open grass field, protection against still frequent Japanese raids, November 1942.* (USMC via Jim Sullivan)

Japanese fighters on even terms, he developed the 'Thach Weave' which proved to be the Wildcat's salvation. A simple manoeuvre, the 'Thach Weave' called for a pair of Wildcats to 'Split-S' toward and away from each other, covering each other in turn. Any enemy fighter that got on the tail of one would be set up for a deflection shot from the other. Word of this new tactic spread quickly through the VFs. It had the advantage of great simplicity and effectiveness, and thus rapidly became standard offensive doctrine, though not in time for the first great carrier battle of the war.

The Japanese drive into the South Pacific took the form of an attempted conquest of Port Moresby, covered by two aircraft carriers. Opposing this move

Fig. 27 *Wildcats continued to be used for area patrol purposes by the Marines after their retirement from front-line fighter units. This was routine work, rarely very exciting, but vital to keeping the sea lanes open. Here a Marine F4F-4 is pushed out of its revetment on Palmyra Island in the Line Island Group, midway between Hawaii and Samoa on the Australian route.* (USMC via Jim Sullivan)

Fig. 28 *BuNo 12228 was the first of the two XF4F-8s, the prototypes for the FM-2 series. Lightened by the removal of two guns and the installation of a Wright Cyclone engine, this version was specifically designed to operate off the small escort carriers. The 'jet' exhaust seen here was retained but the slotted flaps were not. The other prominent feature of the FM-2, the heightened rudder, was introduced on the second prototype.* (Grumman)

were *Lexington* and *Yorktown*, and their Wildcats. As the complex Battle of the Coral Sea developed, the enemy carrier groups groped for each other, finally making contact on 7 May 1942. In the first naval battle in which the opposing vessels never saw each other, the F4F-3s of VF-2 and VF-42 engaged Zeros off Shokaku and Zuikaku. Tactically the battle was a draw, but the Japanese drive into the South Pacific was blunted, making it a definite strategic victory for the US Navy.

One of the lessons learned at Coral Sea was the need for more fighters in each carrier air group. One normal squadron was not big enough to both protect the carrier and escort the attacking bombers. When *Yorktown*, *Hornet* and *Enterprise* sailed to meet the massive Japanese thrust at Midway, it was with the enlarged fighter squadrons. VF-3 on *Yorktown* now had 25 F4F-4s, compared to the 22 F4F-3s of VF-2 which flew off the same carrier at Coral Sea. VF-6 on *Enterprise* and VF-8 on *Hornet* each had 27. The effectiveness of this change is hard to discern from the Midway battle, which was singularly disjointed and decided more by luck than by strategy. Nevertheless, the trend toward larger VFs continued. By July, VF-6 had grown to 36 Wildcats.

While two more carrier battles remained to be fought in 1942, Eastern Solomons in August and Santa Cruz in October, and while Wildcats would fly cover for the invasion of North Africa (Operation *Torch*) in November, the day of the Wildcat as a first-line carrier fighter was rapidly coming to an end. As armour, self-sealing tanks and extra armament were added to the basic Wildcat, performance gradually declined while the quality of its opposition increased. As early as 1941, Grumman had proposed fitting the Wildcat with a Pratt & Whitney R-2000 engine, an uprated Twin Wasp, but the US Navy rightly perceived that any performance gain would have been marginal and not worth the effort. Another proposal, employing a P&W R-2800 Double Wasp, aroused more interest. The US Navy, however, insisted on a number of other alterations to the Wildcat at the same

time. The end result was to be the F6F Hellcat which began to replace the Wildcats on the fleet's carriers in mid-1943. In the meanwhile, there was to be a lot more action for the F4F, but the scene now shifts from the wooden decks of the fleet carriers to a sandy airstrip on a miserable island in the South Pacific.

Guadalcanal, a steamy jungle island in the Solomons chain, became important only because the Japanese began to build an airstrip there in the aftermath of the Coral Sea battle. The threat such an airfield could pose to the Australian 'lifeline' was terrible to contemplate, terrible enough to force the Allies into immediate action. On 7 August 1942, the 1st Marine Division neatly captured the almost-finished airstrip, making it available as an emergency landing field for the F4Fs of VF-6 that were covering the landing. The first permanent residents at the newly-christened Henderson Field were the 19 F4F-4s of VMF-223 which arrived on 20 August. They were just the first of many. Guadalcanal proved to be a 'meatgrinder', wiping out the cream of the Japanese Navy's pilot corps and effectively decimating at least four Marine fighter squadrons.

VMF-223 lasted less than a week in the 'meatgrinder', but, except for its brevity, its story was typical. Four days after it arrived, it saw its first major combat, engaging 19 Bettys and 12 Zekes from Rabaul. Sixteen enemy planes were claimed, including half of the Zeros, but it cost four Wildcats. Such ratios were typical. The Japanese consistently lost many more aircraft than they brought down, but they stubbornly came back day after day, wearing down the Marines in the process. By the 26th, VMF-223 was down to three operational aircraft and was replaced by VMF-224. As Japanese losses in the South Pacific mounted, the intensity of the combat gradually slackened, but it continued at a desperate pace well into early 1943. VMF-224 lasted through most of September before it was in turn replaced by VMF-121. The 121 squadron was joined in early October by VMF-212, as Henderson Field was enlarged to handle a second unit. Before the campaign was over, two more

Fig. 29 & 30 *The US Navy reserved its best pilots for the fleet carriers, meaning that the VCs (Composite Squadrons made up of Wildcats and Avengers) on the escort carriers were manned by Marines. Reservists or 'green' pilots fresh out of flight school. Add this to the jeep carrier's small flight deck and the result was an increased accident rate. Only the docile slow-speed handling of the Wildcat kept this from being a disaster. Here a Marine unit is qualifying on a 'baby flat top'. M25 is coming in 'high and hot', but will probably catch a later wire. M19 has missed all the wires and is headed for the barrier.* (Jim Sullivan)

Marine squadrons, VMF-112 and VMF-122, would pass through the 'meatgrinder' as well.

Medals of Honor proliferated in those days, as exceptional heroics seemed almost commonplace, still a few incidents stand out. On 16 October, Lt Col H W 'Indian Joe' Bauer, CO of VMF-212, while protecting the landing of his squadron which had just flown up from Efate, shot down four out of nine Vals that were attempting an attack on the airfield. On 23 October, Capt Joe Foss of VMF-121 shot down four Zekes and repeated the feat three days later. By 15 January, Foss had equalled Eddie Rickenbacker's WW1 record of 26 victories, the first American to do so.

The fighting ended on Guadalcanal in February 1943, but the Solomons campaign was to stretch on into 1944. Those later island battles would be largely fought without the Wildcat, however, as F4Us rapidly replaced F4Fs in the Marine squadrons beginning in February. Even this didn't mark the end of the Wildcat story, however, as one more field of combat remained for the stubby veteran. Escort carriers had been coming from US shipyards starting in 1941, but because the first ones were committed to the Battle of the Atlantic, their impact in the Pacific wasn't felt until 1943. Originally conceived as 'jeep carriers' which would do nothing more than act as a floating aircraft reserve for their big sisters, their experience in the Atlantic proved that they had great offensive and defensive potential on their own. Gradually the idea evolved of forming task groups of escort carriers attached to a landing force, to provide CAP for the assault fleet and continuous air support for the ground troops, freeing the fleet carriers for strategic operations. Thus, in 1942, the US Navy established the requirement for a lightweight fighter specifically for operation off escort carriers.

Grumman responded with the XF4F-8. Every effort was made to lighten the basic Wildcat. Because little need was seen for high-altitude performance, a Wright R-1820-56 Cyclone with a single-stage supercharger was proposed in the place of the heavier Twin Wasp. The Cyclone provided 1,350hp for take-off but only 1,000hp at 17,500ft (5334m). As a further weight-saving measure, wing armament was to be reduced from three to two .50 machine guns. The design was accepted by the Navy and two prototypes were ordered, but the F4F-8 was never to be mass-produced by Grumman.

The marvel of the American armaments industry in WW2 was its ability to apply expertise in one area to other, seemingly unrelated, fields. No finer example ex-

ists than the Eastern Aircraft Co. With the switching of the American economy from peace to wartime status, General Motors, the largest mass-producer of automobiles in the world, found itself with six unused assembly plants along the east coast. GM proposed setting up an aircraft production company to apply its mass-production experience to the serious aircraft supply problem. The Navy immediately accepted GM's proposal to avert an impending crisis at Grumman. Not only was Grumman producing the Wildcat, but they had also won the competition to design a successor to the TBD Devastator and were working on the Wildcat's replacement. Unable to handle the TBF on top of Wildcat production, Grumman eagerly handed over responsibility for the Avenger to Eastern in 1941. When the Navy accepted the F6F as the Wildcat's successor, the same problem arose. This time, rather than giving production-responsibility for the new aircraft to Eastern, Grumman chose to retain the Hellcat and turn over the F4F. Thus in 1942, Eastern accepted responsibility for F4F-4 production. Absolutely identical to the F4F-4, the first FM-1 came off the assembly line in late 1942. So it was, in 1943, that when the Navy accepted Grumman's proposal for a lightened Wildcat, all production examples came from Eastern Aircraft Co as FM-2s.

The two XF4F-8s (Bu Nos 12228 & '9) exhibited a number of new features for a Wildcat. Both had slotted flaps, a feature which proved disappointing and wasn't included in the production version, and direct exhaust ejection for improved performance. The most noticeable feature of the FM-2, the enlarged rudder, showed up only on the second prototype. The first FM-2 came off the Linden, New Jersey, production line in 1943, entering fleet service before the end of the year. Production tempo increased rapidly. Only 310 were produced in 1943, but 2,890 were put together the next year.

By the time the great Central Pacific offensive began in mid-1944, FM-2s on escort carriers were an essential part of the assault plan. The FM-2 proved to be a popular fighter, simple and easy to handle, ideally suited for the often inexperienced pilots assigned to the escort carrier VCs (Composite Squadrons). Although it was less heavily armed and had inferior altitude performance in comparison to an F4F-4, the FM-2, because it was lighter, had far superior climb and manoeuvrability.

It is ironic that perhaps the finest moment for this

often overmatched fighter should come now when its primary job was done and it had been relegated to 'second-line' duties. Yet, long after the tide had turned in the Pacific, when the question was not if but when victory would occur, the Wildcat, in its latest reincarnation, would stave off one final disaster.

Dawn on 25 October 1944 promised another 'usual' day for the six escort carriers of Rear Adml Clifton Sprague's Taffy 3. GIs were fighting for a beachhead on Leyte, and Taffy 3 would spend another day providing close air support for them and the invasion fleet. They were ideally positioned, covering the northern approaches to Leyte. Two sister units, Taffy 1 and Taffy 2, were off Mindanao and directly east of Leyte Gulf, providing similar support. Every sailor knew that the Japanese were throwing everything they had at this first landing in the Philippines. A huge battleship armada had been routed by the Helldivers and Avengers of Halsey's TF38 and was last seen in full retreat. A smaller force had sailed right into Oldendorf's battle line just the night before and had ceased to exist. And now the last of the Japanese aircraft carriers had been spotted way to the north and Halsey was off in hot pursuit. The Japanese Navy appeared to be receiving a final drubbing. Except that Ozawa's carrier force off Cape Engano was a decoy designed to lure Halsey away and Kurita's force of battleships and cruisers, despite the fearful pounding they had received the day before, had turned around again at dusk and was now barrelling down on the invasion fleet.

The Japanese dream, the American's greatest nightmare, a battle fleet loose among the invasion transports, seemed about to be coming true. Only Taffy 3, with about 97 FM-2s and 72 Avengers, stood in between. Six thin-skinned escort carriers, three destroyers and four destroyer escorts stood in the path of four battleships, eight cruisers and 11 destroyers. It should have been a rout, but it wasn't. Seemingly every element favoured the Japanese. They had even approached to nearly gunfire range without being detected, but still they were unable to break through because, as they themselves had so ably proved nearly three years before, the day of the battlefleet without air cover was over.

Luck certainly helped Taffy 3 that morning. Taffy 1 had already launched its morning strikes, but Taffy 3 was running a little slow and still had most of its aircraft on deck. Most of Taffy 2's aircraft were in the air and were immediately diverted to Sprague's assistance. And most luckily, a rain squall developed into which Taffy 3 could disappear for 25 blessed minutes, changing course, picking up speed and launching aircraft. Nevertheless, by 07.30 the squall was left behind and Kurita's battlefleet was well within gunfire range. The next 90 minutes told the tale. Every time a cruiser or battleship got close, it was swarmed by Wildcats and Avengers. At first they had been able to land back on the carriers when they were out of torpedoes or ammo, but now the flattops were dodging shells and, anyway, they had long since depleted their magazines. So the pilots did what they had to do. Time and again they made 'dry runs' on Kurita's leading cruisers, forcing them to twist and turn, disturbing their aim. (One FM-2 pilot made 20 'strafing' runs that day, 10 of them after his ammo was gone.) Enough of Taffy 2's fresh aircraft were mixed in to keep the Japanese 'honest'. Four TBMs off Taffy 3's *Kitkun Bay* teamed up to mortally wound *Chokai* and Taffy 2's Wildcats and Avengers sent *Chikuma* to the bottom.

Despite these incredible efforts, the Japanese were gaining. By 09.00, Kurita's cruisers had almost reached pointblank range. *Gambier Bay* was caught and holed, sinking at 09.07. The rest couldn't last too much longer. Then fortune smiled one last crucial time. At this critical moment, Kurita, hounded by the incessant attacks of the, now largely unarmed, Wildcats and Avengers, presumed his damage to be greater than it actually was, lost his nerve and called off the attack. The Japanese made good their retreat, escaping westward long before Halsey could intervene. Taffy 3 survived by luck and the desperate skill of its pilots. (Its luck ran out that same afternoon, as *St Lo* was hit by one of the war's first kamikazes and sank). Most importantly, the invasion fleet never left Leyte Gulf.

Now the Wildcat's postscript can finally be written. FM-2s served out the war, covering the remaining invasions of Iwo Jima and Okinawa, but the end of the war saw the end of the Wildcat's era. Few escort carriers would be needed in a peacetime Navy, and those that did survive would need newer fighters. The ten years that had passed had seen a revolution in aircraft design, and the Wildcat no longer fitted in. Never spectacular, but always available, the Wildcat did its job. There can be no finer memorial than that.

Fig. 31 & 32 *FM-2s operating off Makin Island in Lingayen Gulf on 8 January 1945 show off the overall Glossy Sea Blue camouflage ordered in October 1944. The exhaust stain coming from the exhaust port at the rear of the cowling stands out against the dark paint.* (USN-NARS)

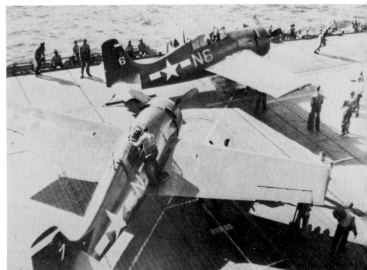

Fig. 33 *One of* **Rudyerd Bay***'s* **Wildcats** *snagged the barrier and nosed down on 1 April 1945. Late-production FM-2s had three rocket stubs under each wing, increasing their potency in the ground support role.* (USN-NARS)

SPECIFICATIONS

XF4F-2

Dimensions: length, 26ft 5in (8052mm); span, 34ft 0in (10363mm); wing area, 232sq ft (21.554sq m).
Weights: gross weight, 5,386lb (2443kg); empty weight, 4,035lb (1830kg).
Performance: max speed at 10,000ft (3048m), 290mph (467km/hr); rate of climb, 2,650ft/min (808m/min); range, 740 miles (1191km); ceiling, 27,400ft (8351m).
Powerplant: Pratt & Whitney R-1830-66 of 1,050hp take-off power (1-stage, 1-speed supercharger).
Armament: 4 × .50 (12.7mm) machine guns.

XF4F-3

Dimensions: length, 28ft 0in (8534mm); span, 38ft 0in (11582mm); wing area, 260sq ft (24.155sq m)
Weights: gross weight, 6,099lb (2767kg), empty weight, 4,863lb (2206kg).
Performance: max speed at 20,500ft (6248m), 334mph (538km/hr); rate of climb, 2,800ft/min (853m/min); range, 907 miles (1460km); ceiling, 33,500ft (10210m).
Powerplant: Pratt & Whitney XR-1830-76 of 1,200hp take-off power (2-stage, 2-speed supercharger).
Armament: 2 × .30 (7.6mm) machine guns; 2 × .50 (12.7mm) machine guns.

F4F-3

Dimensions: length, 28ft 9in (8763mm); span, 38ft 0in (11582mm); wing area, 260sq ft (24.155sq m).
Weights: gross weight, 7,065lb (3205kg); empty weight, 5,238lb (2376Kg).
Performance: max speed at 21,300ft (6492m), 331mph (533km/hr); rate of climb, 2,300ft/min (701m/min); range, 860miles (1384km); ceiling, 37,000ft (11277m).
Powerplant: Pratt & Whitney R-1830-76/86 of 1,200hp take-off power (2-stage, 2-speed supercharger).
Armament: 4 × .50 machine guns.

F4F-3A

Dimensions: length, 28ft 9in (8763mm); span, 38ft 0in (11582mm); wing area, 260sq ft (24.155sq m).
Weights: gross weight, 6,876lb (3119kg); empty weight, 5,216lb (2366kg).
Performance: max speed at 16,000ft (4877m), 312mph (502km/hr); rate of climb, 2,430ft/min; (741m/min); range, 825 miles (1328km); ceiling, 34,300ft (10454m).
Powerplant: Pratt & Whitney R-1830-90 of 1,200hp take-off power (1-stage, 2-speed supercharger).
Armament: 4 × .50 machine guns.

F4F-4

Dimensions: length, 28ft 9in (8763mm); span, 38ft 0in (11582mm); wing area, 260sq ft (24.155sq m)
Weights: gross weight, 7,964lb (3612kg); empty weight, 5,766lb (2615kg).
Performance: max speed at 19,400ft (5913m), 318mph (512km/hr); rate of climb, 2,190ft/min (668m/min); ceiling, 33,700ft (10271m).
Powerplant: Pratt & Whitney R-1830-86 of 1,200hp take-off power (2-stage, 2-speed supercharger).
Armament: 6 × .50 (12.7mm) machine guns.

FM-2

Dimensions: length, 28ft 11in (8814mm); span, 38ft 0in (11582mm); wing area, 260sq ft (24.155sq m).
Weights: gross weight, 7,431lb (3371kg); empty weight, 5,542lb (2514kg).
Performance: max speed at 16,800 (5121m), 320mph (515km/hr); rate of climb, 2,890ft/min (881m/min); ceiling, 35,600ft (10851m).
Powerplant: Wright R-1820-56 of 1,350hp take-off power (1-stage, 2-speed supercharger).
Armament: 4 × .50 (12.7mm) machine guns.

GRUMMAN F6F HELLCAT

Fig. 1 *An image of power, roaring Double Wasps spinning huge props as a VF-83 Hellcat gets the go, while another warms up in the foreground. Essex's F6F-5s carried a yellow cowl band during operations off Iwo Jima, February 1945.* (USN-NARS)

Fig. 2 *The differences between the XF6F-1, seen here, and the last production F6F-5 were remarkably few and minor. Note the broad exhaust port behind the cowling, which is the sole distinction between the Cyclone- and Double Wasp-powered prototypes. This airframe (BuNo 02981) was later converted into XF6F-3 configuration, later still was the sole XF6F-4 and finally was delivered as a standard F6F-3.* (Grumman)

No sooner had the F4F Wildcat finally entered service with the US Navy in late 1940, than work began to produce an improved version. Despite the many fine qualities of the F4F-3s then coming off the production line, the Wildcat had been designed to a specification already five years old in 1940 and held a questionable superiority over possible carrier-borne opponents and was definitely inferior to land-based contemporaries. Not too many years before that inferiority had been accepted as normal, but the introduction of the Mitsubishi A5M1 Claude by the Japanese in 1936 had proven that carrier aircraft could indeed match their land-based opponents and navies had come to expect at least equal performance from their carrier fighters. Moreover, the first sketchy reports were arriving from China of a new Japanese naval fighter with performance so incredible that the reports were presumed to be grossly exagerated. Nevertheless, it was obvious that should war break out with Japan, considered inevitable by most US naval planners, an improved Wildcat would be very useful, if not essential, in the battle for the Pacific.

The improvements desired by BuAer in the new Wildcat involved virtually every aspect of a fighter's performance. The Navy wanted the new version to have better power with resultant higher top speed and improved manoeuvrability, greater range, more armour and more ammunition. Grumman was hardly surprised by the Navy's request. Indeed, they had already proposed one Wildcat upgrade powered by the Pratt & Whitney R-2000 Twin Wasp which had been rejected because it offered insufficient improvement to make an interruption of production worthwhile. A second Grumman proposal for an F4F powered by the new Wright R-2600 Cyclone of 1500hp, a 14-cylinder version of the R-1820 9-cylinder radial, was accepted on 30 June 1941.

While the Navy and Grumman had been thinking up to this point in terms of an improved Wildcat, both soon realised that the desired improvements could not be achieved by simply hanging a bigger engine on the front of an F4F airframe. The requirement for greater fuel capacity and more armour demanded a bigger fuselage. Similarly, the requirement for improved manoeuvrability and greater ammo stowage could only be achieved with a larger wing. Obviously a total redesign was in order.

What emerged was the XF6F-1 which flew for the first time on 26 July 1942. Many stories have circulated to the effect that the F6F was designed specifically to master the Mitsubishi A6M2 Zero, that its design was recast in the light of reports of the Zero's performance. This is largely fanciful. Reports had indeed been arriving from Stilwell and Chennault in China accurately describing the Zero's abilities since mid-1940, but Stilwell was an Army officer and Chennault was considered a publicity-seeking crank and the reports were ignored. When the accuracy of their reports was proven in the skies over Hawaii, the Phillipines, Burma and Indonesia, the sole XF6F-1 was already under construction. (The first Zero to fall intact into allied hands would be captured only about the time of the XF6F-1's first flight and would not be available for flight testing for months to come.)

The XF6F-1 bore a family resemblance to the Wildcat it was designed to replace, but a side-by-side comparison revealed considerable differences, particularly in size. The XF6F-1 was 33ft 7in (10236mm) in length compared to 28ft 9in (8763mm) for the Wildcat. The prototype's wingspan was 42ft 10 in (13056mm) compared to 38ft 0in (11582mm) for the Wildcat. At 334sq ft, (31sq m) the XF6F-1 had a bigger wing than any other US single-seat fighter. Construction was entirely conventional, identical to that of the Wildcat. Stressed aluminium skin was flush-riveted to an all-metal semi-monocoque frame. Tail control surfaces were metal framed with fabric covering. The most noticeable change from the Wildcat was the adoption of a "conventional" landing gear in the place of the short-stroke belly-mounted landing gear of the Wildcat. The decision to use a rearward-retracting wing-mounted landing gear in turn led to the adoption of a low-wing in the place of the Wildcat's mid-wing. This had the additonal advantage of improving the pilot's downward vision.

From its first flight, the XF6F-1 (BuNo 02981) had all the marks of a successful design. To the delight of the Navy, the prototype proved to be stable and easy to fly. Some minor tail flutter was cleared up by strengthening the aft structure. If anything, the prototype was too stable. Considerable effort was required to move it off

Fig. 3 The XF6F-3s differed from a standard '-3' mainly in the spinner, which was deleted on production aircraft, and landing gear doors, which were reduced in size. This is the original XF6F-1 in one of its temporary guises. (Grumman)

Fig. 4 *An early production F6F-3 makes shaky landing on* Cowpens *in November 1943. VF-6 was one of the squadrons that took the Hellcat into its first action, the Gilberts Campaign.* (USN via NHS)

the straight and level until a minor revision of the ailerons solved the problem. Once these bugs were worked out, the XF6F-1 rapidly completed an otherwise uneventful test sequence. Range, manoeuvrability and gunpower all more than met the Navy's requirements. Only power disappointed BuAer. Here, for the first time, knowledge of the Zero's performance influenced the design of the Hellcat. The prototype had a top speed of 375mph (604km/hr) compared to 340mph (547km/hr) for the A6M2. While this may have seemed a comfortable margin, the Navy was concerned about the future. Their new fighter not only had to be faster than the current generation of enemy fighters, it also would have to beat future upgrades or replacements. With the additional incentive of simplifying supply lines, the Navy requested that Grumman replace the XF6F-1's R-2600 with the Pratt & Whitney R-2800-10 Double Wasp 2000hp radial which was already powering the F4U Corsair. The 500hp increase in horsepower was expected to augment the XF6F's top speed and also im-

prove the rate of climb, which had also disappointed the Navy.

The second prototype (BuNo 02982), which was to have been completed as the XF6F-2 powered by a turbo-supercharged Cyclone, was hurriedly re-engined with a Double Wasp in time to fly on 30 July 1942. The XF6F-3, as the second prototype was designated, was physically identical to the XF6F-1, except for the change of engine and some revision to the exhaust ports on either side. The ''-3'' retained all of the good qualities of the first prototype with some significant improvements in performance. The XF6F-3's top speed was 385mph (620km/hr). Even more significantly, the rate of climb increased from 2350ft/min (716m/min) to 3100ft/min (945m/min). (This would be the only area in which the F6F was inferior to the Zero, which climbed at 4500ft/min (1372m/min).) The Navy proclaimed itself pleased with its new fighter, now dubbed Hellcat, which was immediately ordered into production. (The time necessary to get a design into production had been

Fig. 5 *51-F-2 skips the barriers enroute to a disastrous encounter with the bridge. Note the forward deckcrew beginning to scatter. Chances were good that the pilot would survive relatively unscathed. The odds for any deckcrewman in the vicinity were considerably slimmer.* (USN via Jim Sullivan)

dramatically shortened from the time when the F4F was at a similar stage of development. The pressure of war had reduced the time from prototype flight to production decision from 17 to 3 months.)

This decision was entirely expected by Grumman, which had already begun making arrangements to transfer responsibility for Wildcat production to Eastern Aircraft Co. The changes in tooling were made in record time and the first production Hellcat (BuNo 04775) flew on 4 October 1942. Except for the replacement of the three-bladed Curtiss Electric propeller by a spinnerless four-bladed Hamilton Standard model, the production F6F-3 was identical to the prototype. In fact, over the life of the Hellcat, spanning some 12,000 examples, it went through fewer changes than any other major production aircraft. For example, the only difference between the first and second production blocks was the substitution of the R-2800-10W (with water injection) for the ''-10'' and the deletion of the underwing landing light. The water-injected engine would be standard

throughout the rest of the Hellcat's production life. There was no difference whatsoever between the second and third blocks.

Carquals showed some unexpected weakness in the rear fuselage of the Hellcat, a number of tail separations occurring on landing. Local strengthening easily solved this final problem and Hellcats were issued to VF-9 off *Essex* in January 1943. VF-9 became the first squadron to take the Hellcat to sea, as they worked up their F6F-3s rapidly and proceded to the Pacific. The honour of being the first squadron to take Hellcats into action fell to VF-5 off *Yorktown*, when they escorted Dauntlesses on a raid on Marcus Is. on 31 August 1943. So rapidly were Hellcats introduced, that all 12 VFs on the 11 fleet and light carriers of TF50, the strike force for the Gilberts Campaign in November 1943, were equipped with F6F-3s. This domination of the carrier decks would remain unchallenged, except for night fighters, until the first Corsair-equipped VFs were assigned to the fleet in late 1944.

Fig. 6. Above   *The Hellcat's finest hour was the Battle of the Phillipine Sea, 19 June 1944. On that day Cdr David McCampbell, CO of CVG-15 off Essex, seen here in his personal mount, 'The Minsi', shot down four Judys and a Zeke in two separate actions. His Hellcat is unusual in its lack of markings. The only indication of its owner's rank is the initials 'AGC' (for Air Group Commander) on the landing gear door.* (USN-NARS)

Fig. 7. Below   *F6F-3s of* **Bunker Hill**'s *VF-8 prepare for launch. The air group markings are the white band above and below the tail number. The same individual aircraft number is repeated in black on the cowl lip and landing gear door. Note the wing roundel which lacks the regulation blue surround, a not uncommon practice at this time, June 1944.* (USN-NARS)

Fig. 8. Above *Deckcrew begins to fold the wing of this VF-2 Hellcat at the time of the Marianas Campaign. CVG-2 (Hornet) aircraft carried a white circle and aircraft-in-group number on the tail, with the number repeated large under the cockpit, June 1944.*

Fig. 9. Below *Pilots mount their Hellcats as VF-2 prepares for a mission. Each of the three F6F-3s in this view has a different style national insignia. No. 2's lacks the regulation blue surround on fuselage as well as upper wing (very rare), No. 38's has a non-regulation glossy sea blue surround (not too unusual at this time – created by the hasty overpainting of the red surround that was standard until September 1943) and No. 37's which is standard insignia blue. The prop bosses are white, June 1944.* (USN-NARS)

Fig. 10 & 11 *When returning aircraft are in the recovery pattern and running low on fuel, absolutely nothing is allowed to interrupt the landing sequence. This was especially true during a battle, as these views of the 'landing' and disposal of VF-1's No. 28 in the midst of the 'Turkey Shoot', 19 June 1944, can attest. The F6F-3 hit the barrier and nosed over, bending prop and wingtip. Under normal circumstances, she would have been taken below and repaired, but now she was just in the way and was unceremoniously dumped off the midships elevator.* (USN-NARS)

Fig. 12 *In less hurried circumstances, wounded birds are treated with care. No. 30 of* **Yorktown's** *VF-1 'Tophatters' with flak-damaged tail and collision-damaged wing is towed and pushed forward to the elevator. CVG-1's markings included a diagonal tail stripe, tail number and white 'K' on the rudder, June 1944.* (USN-NARS)

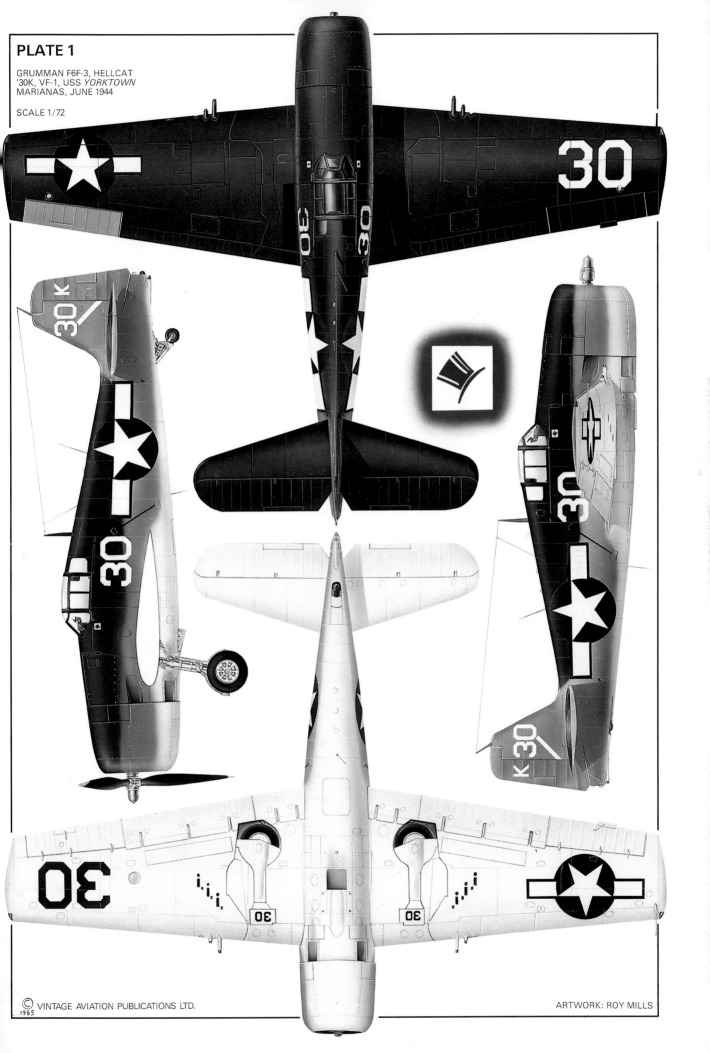

PLATE 1

GRUMMAN F6F-3, HELLCAT
'30K, VF-1, USS *YORKTOWN*
MARIANAS, JUNE 1944

SCALE 1/72

ARTWORK: ROY MILLS

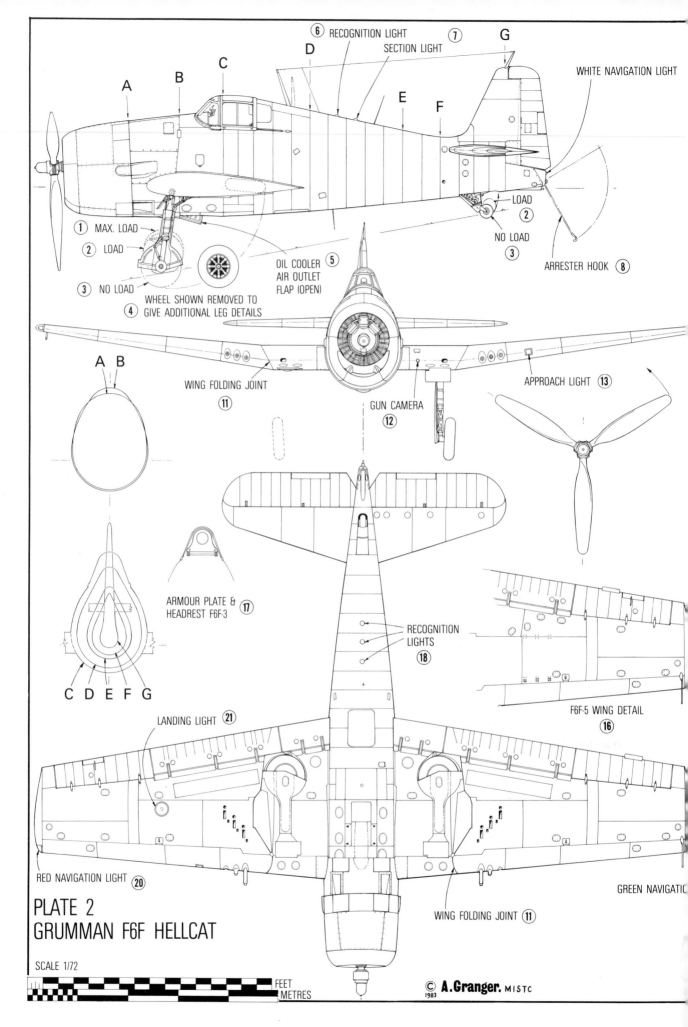

(6) RECOGNITION LIGHT
SECTION LIGHT
(7)

WHITE NAVIGATION LIGHT

A   B   C   D   E   F   G

(1) MAX. LOAD
(2) LOAD
(3) NO LOAD
(4) WHEEL SHOWN REMOVED TO GIVE ADDITIONAL LEG DETAILS

OIL COOLER AIR OUTLET FLAP (OPEN) (5)

LOAD (2)
NO LOAD (3)

ARRESTER HOOK (8)

WING FOLDING JOINT (11)

GUN CAMERA (12)

APPROACH LIGHT (13)

A   B

ARMOUR PLATE & HEADREST F6F-3 (17)

RECOGNITION LIGHTS (18)

F6F-5 WING DETAIL (16)

C   D   E   F   G

LANDING LIGHT (21)

RED NAVIGATION LIGHT (20)

WING FOLDING JOINT (11)

GREEN NAVIGATIO

PLATE 2
GRUMMAN F6F HELLCAT

SCALE 1/72

FEET
METRES

© A.Granger. MISTC
1983

56

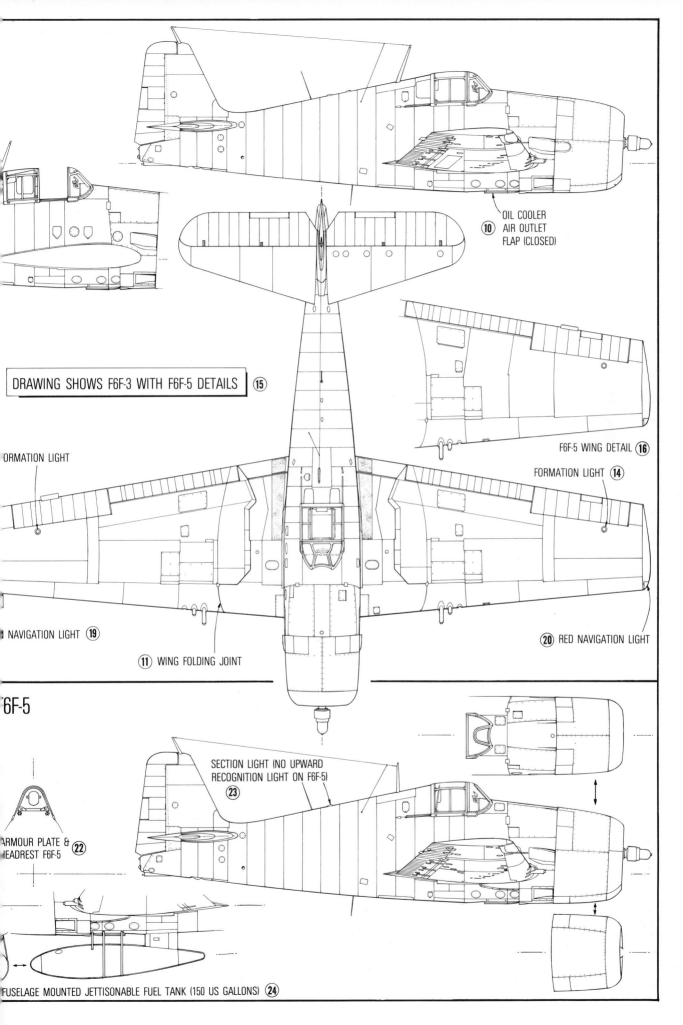

OIL COOLER
(10) AIR OUTLET
FLAP (CLOSED)

DRAWING SHOWS F6F-3 WITH F6F-5 DETAILS (15)

F6F-5 WING DETAIL (16)

ORMATION LIGHT

FORMATION LIGHT (14)

NAVIGATION LIGHT (19)

(20) RED NAVIGATION LIGHT

(11) WING FOLDING JOINT

6F-5

SECTION LIGHT (NO UPWARD
RECOGNITION LIGHT ON F6F-5)
(23)

ARMOUR PLATE &
HEADREST F6F-5 (22)

FUSELAGE MOUNTED JETTISONABLE FUEL TANK (150 US GALLONS) (24)

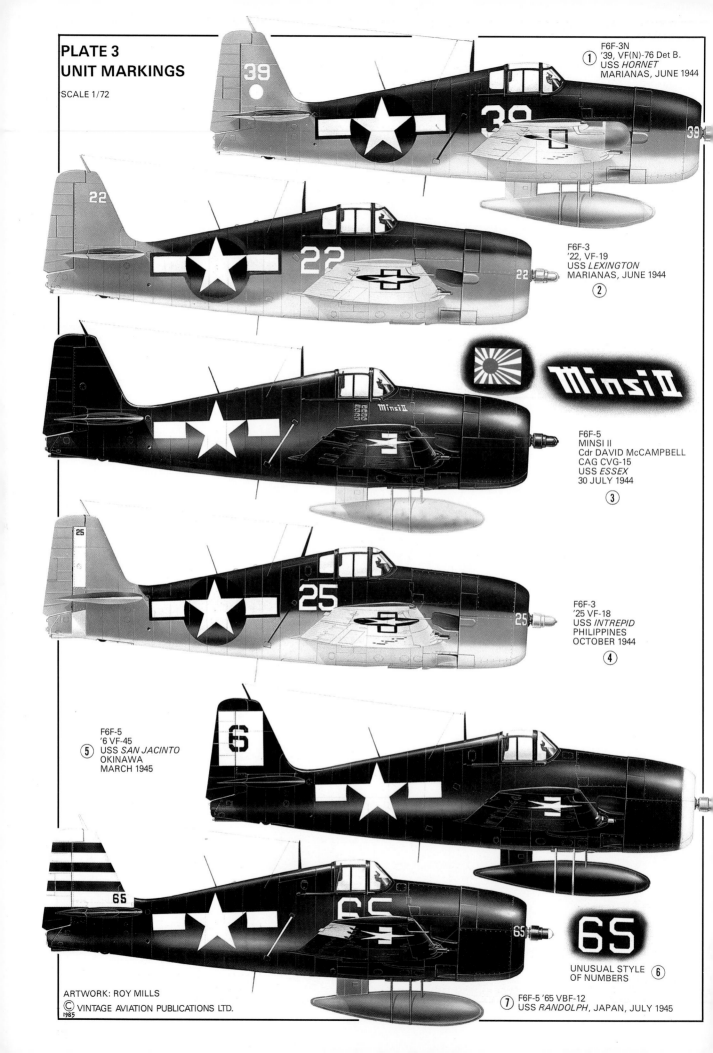

PLATE 3
UNIT MARKINGS

SCALE 1/72

F6F-3N
① '39, VF(N)-76 Det B.
USS *HORNET*
MARIANAS, JUNE 1944

F6F-3
'22, VF-19
USS *LEXINGTON*
MARIANAS, JUNE 1944
②

F6F-5
MINSI II
Cdr DAVID McCAMPBELL
CAG CVG-15
USS *ESSEX*
30 JULY 1944
③

F6F-3
'25 VF-18
USS *INTREPID*
PHILIPPINES
OCTOBER 1944
④

F6F-5
⑤ '6 VF-45
USS *SAN JACINTO*
OKINAWA
MARCH 1945

UNUSUAL STYLE
OF NUMBERS ⑥

F6F-5 '65 VBF-12
⑦ USS *RANDOLPH*, JAPAN, JULY 1945

ARTWORK: ROY MILLS

© VINTAGE AVIATION PUBLICATIONS LTD.
1985

The F6F-5 differs from the F6F-3 in the following respects:
1. Oil cooler shutter control.
2. Fuselage droppable tank manual release control.
3. Anti-blackout regulator.
4. Intercooler shutter control.
5. Removal of the fuel level warning light.

Fig. 14 *Cockpit – port side* (Grumman)

Fig. 15 *Cockpit – starboard side* (Grumman)

The F6F-5 differs from the F6F-3 in the following respects:
1. Generator warning light.
2. IFF destructor switch.
3. Radio master control switch.
4. Rocket projectile arming switch.
5. IFF controls.

Fig. 16 *Rearming a Hellcat was a remarkably simple operation, because of the rearward-folding wings. No. 3's wing number is interesting. The overspray shows that the markings were spray-painted on through masking tape templates. For unknown reasons, this number is upside-down. Wing numbers were supposed to be read from the trailing edge, VF-1,* Yorktown, *June 1944.* (USN-NARS)

Although the Hellcat had not been designed specifically to beat the Zero, that is exactly what it did. A Hellcat pilot felt he could take on Zeroes at any time and win. The Hellcat was faster at all altitudes (375mph (604km/hr) at 20,000ft (6096m) vs. 346mph (557km/hr) for the Zero 53c — the ultimate production variant which appeared in 1945), could outdive Zekes with ease, could stay with a Zero in most manoeuvres, in fact could do everything as well or better except climb. On top of these performance advantages, the Hellcat pilot had 200lbs (91kg) of armour and self-sealing tanks. The Zero 53c had only armour glass but did also have self-sealing fuel tanks. (It was the only Zeke variant to have this feature. Some earlier models had automatic fire extinguishers which proved absolutely ineffective. Zeroes more than earned their reputation of being easy to set on fire.) It took a brave pilot to fly any model Zero against Hellcats and a very good one to do so with success.

The Hellcat would dominate the skies in which it flew from the day of its introduction well into 1945, but its

heyday was 1944. Its finest hour probably was the "Great Marianas Turkey Shoot". The real turning point of the Pacific Campaign, the Battle of the Phillipine Sea on 19 June 1944 utterly and finally destroyed Japanese naval air power. The Japanese launched 324 attacking aircraft at Spruance's TF58, with its 14 Hellcat-equipped VFs (with 443 F6F-3 day fighters on strength) and lost at least 217 in air combat against the loss of 22 Hellcats. Never again would Japanese carrier aviation be a factor in the war.

Very early in the Hellcat's service life, the need was perceived for specialised variants to fill specific needs of the fleet. In particular, a demand was made for Hellcat's modified to carry the newly-developed radar equipment just being introduced. Hence the F6F-3E/N. The 18 F6F-3Es were equipped with AN/APS-4 sea search radar in a pod slung under the starboard wing. No more "-3Es" were built because APS-4-equipped SBDs were becoming available, which were better suited for the sea search role. On the other hand, 205 F6F-3Ns were completed, equipped with AN/APS-6 air search radar in a pod faired into the leading edge of the starboard wing. Both versions were otherwise externally identical to the standard day fighter Hellcat, retaining full armament and ammunition stowage. Both had similar revisions to cockpit instrumentation, normal flight gauges being moved aside to make room for the large radar display in the centre of the instrument panel. The F6F-3N was a successful and popular variant which was succeeded on production lines by the nearly identical F6F-5N.

The first hints of discontent from the fleet about the performance of the F6F-3 began to be heard in mid-1944. The Japanese had entered WW2 with an edge in aircraft performance but quickly lost that lead as new US types arrived on the scene. Apparently planning on a short war, they failed to have the successors to their early Zekes and Oscars in production much before 1944, giving US designers a significant breathing space. Nevertheless, the first examples of "second-generation" Japanese combat aircraft began to be en-

countered by fleet aircraft in mid-1944. Tojos, with a top speed only 10mph (16km/hr) less than the Hellcat's, had begun to appear in mid-1943, but they were Army fighters and did not encounter Hellcats too frequently. The first of the new naval fighters was the Jack (Mitsubishi J2M2), first encountered over Guam in June 1944. Early Jacks shared the Zero's fault of being too lightly armed and armoured (the first action reports claimed that they burned just as easily as Zekes), but they were significantly faster. Though still not available in large quantities, it seemed to bode ill for the future that the Japanese now had production fighters only marginally inferior to the F6F-3 in performance.

Work had begun on an improved Hellcat even before the F6F-3 entered production but progress was slow due to the importance of getting the Hellcat into service. A turbo-supercharged XF6F-2 was under construction in 1941 but was taken over on the line to become the first XF6F-3. As the initial complaints about the "-3s" performance began to be heard, the idea was dusted off and

Fig. 17 *CVG markings were unofficial until finally codified by the Navy on 7 October 1944. Because of delays in implementation, nearly all aircraft retained their old markings through the Phillipines Campaign; Here No. 4 of* Lexington's *VF-19 launches. None of VF-19s Hellcats carried the CVG-19 hollow triangle insignia. Instead, they repeated the aircraft number behind the cockpit, a position unique to this squadron, 10 October 1944.* (USN-NARS)

Fig. 18 *The transition to the 'Geometric Symbols' caused considerable confusion as squadrons were re-marked only as time allowed. Here a flak-damaged F6F-3 of* Intrepid's *VF-18 displays its new insignia, a vertical white stripe, on 25 October 1944. This marking was also the 'old' insignia of* Cabot's *CVG-29, which happened to be in the same task group (TG38.2) during the Phillipines Campaign. Confusion between the air groups was constant until the changeover was completed in January 1945.* (USN-NARS)

BuNo 66244, the last F6F-3 in the fourth production block, was taken over in September 1943 and converted into the XF6F-2. Powered initially by an R-2600-15 linked to a Birmann turbo-supercharger (driven by exhaust gas rather than mechanically driven in the case of a standard supercharger), and later by a similarly boosted R-2800-21, the experiment did improve high altitude performance significantly but did not help at medium altitudes where most combats occurred. Any improvement was considered too minor to warrant a

change in the production standard, and the sole prototype was converted back to a normal day fighter and delivered to the fleet.

There was also a single XF6F-4, actually the original XF6F-1 (BuNo 02981) which had been modified into the second XF6F-3, reconverted to carry cannon armament. Fitted with four 20mm cannons in the place of the six .50s and an uprated R-2800-27, the revised prototype flew for the first time in this configuration on 3 October 1942. While this exact model never went into produc-

Fig. 19 *The XF6F-2, originally projected in June 1942, was finally built in December 1943. Named 'Fuzzy Wuzzy' because of the wool strings applied over its surface to show air flow, the XF6F-2 was a standard '-3' (BuNo 66244) which was fitted with a turbo-supercharged R-2600-15, later replaced by an R-2800-21. The only changes from 'standard' were the deepened cowling and four-bladed, spinnered prop.* (Grumman)

Fig. 20 *Because of the great similarity of the '-5' to the '-3', the transition from the old to the new was gradual. F6F-3s continued to serve until they would normally have been replaced. One of the earliest '-5s' to reach the fleet, an F6F-5N of VF(N)-77 Det A, prepares to launch off* Essex *on 10 May 1944.* (USN-NARS)

Fig. 21 *Cdr David McCampbell replaced 'The Minsi' with an overall glossy sea blue F6F-5, 'Minsi II', seen here undergoing extensive maintenance onboard* Essex, *30 July 1944. Again, McCampbell's aircraft is almost unmarked except for personal markings, victory flags and 'CAG' (the more standard acronym for Air Group CO) on the gear door. The odd-looking contraption hanging behind the prop is used for boresighting the guns.* (USN-NARS)

Fig. 22. Above *The transition of markings and camouflage late in 1944 created some interesting paradoxes. Compare the pair of sea blue VF-18 F6F-5s seen here on* **Intrepid**, *25 October 1944, with the three-tone SB2C seen above on the same day. The overall glossy sea blue camouflage, authorised on the same day as the standardised geometric insignia, has been applied to this pair, which retain CVG-18's old-style white cross marking.   SB2C above has the new marking but retains the old camouflage.* (USN-NARS)

Fig. 23. Below *Another example of old markings on new camouflage is this F6F-5 seen on* **Lexington** *on 26 October 1944. No. 22 has snagged the barrier, dinging the prop, cowling and belly tank. Fire crew and first aid team stand by as the pilot is helped from the cockpit.* (USN-NARS)

Fig. 24 & 25 *Two views of No. 91, an F6F-5 off* **Ticonderoga,** *catching a late wire. It did not take long for exhaust stains to ruin a pristine overall glossy sea blue finish. This is a standard F6F-5, as can be ascertained by noting two normally hard-to-see features, the paired trim tabs on the ailerons and the reduced framing in the forward canopy, October 1944.* (USN-NARS)

tion, the cannon experiments were considered a success, and a mixed cannon-machine gun armament was adopted as alternate standard on F6F-5s and as standard on F6F-5Ns. BuNo 02981 went through a fourth metamorphosis and was delivered back to the Navy as a standard F6F-3.

A new Hellcat version did indeed supplant the "-3" on Grumman's assembly line in Spring 1944, although most pilots probably never noticed the difference. It was most definitely not the improved Hellcat that the fleet was requesting. The Navy had decided that Hellcat production should not be interrupted at this time for a major model change. There were at least two main reasons for this decision. BuAer was still undecided as to whether the Hellcat or the Vought Corsair would be its main carrier fighter for the foreseeable future. Additionally, there appeared to be another, different, Grumman in the Navy's future. Two prototypes of the new, much anticipated, XF8F-1 had been ordered in late 1943. These factors combined to rule out any major development of the Hellcat design at this time. Yet, with the carrier fleet still growing at a fast pace, Hellcats would be needed for quite some time, no matter which fighter was chosen as the new standard. The Navy approved the changeover to the F6F-5 to begin in April 1944.

So similar was the "-5" to the "-3" that no prototype was considered necessary. Most of the changes that are normally considered recognition features of the F6F-5 actually were made before or after model changeover. A mid-production F6F-5 can be distinguished from an early F6F-3 by a number of differences, including the suppression of the lower cowl flaps and lateral exhaust bulges in the cowling (change actually made in the fifth block of F6F-3s), deletion of aft canopy windows and dorsal recognition light (change not made until second block of F6F-5s) and provision for six 5" (127mm) HVAR rockets underwing (introduced two months before changeover). The only alterations that coincided exactly with the change in designation were more subtle and difficult to see. These included the addition of a second trim tab on each aileron, the provision for mixed cannon/machine gun armament (almost never seen on day fighters) and adoption of integral rather than separate armour glass in the windscreen. This last was the most definite recognition feature of the F6F-5. The new forward canopy lacked the characteristic lateral brace on either side. The "-5" also included provision

for carrying two 250gal (946lt) external tanks or 2×1000lb (454kg) bombs underwing. Power was provided by the same R-2800-10W and performance was virtually identical. 7820 of the new version were completed by Grumman before production ended in November 1945. Of these, 753 went to the Royal Navy.

A series of variants on the basic F6F-5 were built, similar to the "-3s". 1529 F6F-5Ns were completed, again with AN/APS-6 radar faired into the leading edge of the starboard wing. Three of these went to the RN. These differed from the standard day fighter in adopting the mixed armament of 2×20mm cannon and 4×.50 machine guns provided for in the basic design. A few early "-5Ns" had exhaust flame dampers, but these were generally dispensed with as they caused some loss in performance. A few F6F-5Ps were completed with a fixed K-18 camera in the portside of the fuselage just behind the wing trailing edge. This modification is almost impossible to see in photos and exact numbers are difficult to ascertain as many were field-modified. It

Fig. 26 *An F6F-5 of* **Hornet's** *VF-17 shows off the CVG-17 markings, white squares quartering the tail and wingtips. This is obviously a lull between operations off Iwo Jima, deckcrewmen lounge on a jeep and deck tractor. As can be seen from the tail plane in the foreground, the glossy sea blue paint was very shiny, at least when fresh.* (USN-NARS)

Fig. 27 & 28 *Among the fanciest of tail markings belonged to* **Randolph**'s *CVG-12, three blue stripes on a white tail and white ailerons. A deckload of F6F-5s of VF-12 and VBF-12 are being launched off the bow catapults during the strikes on the Japanese mainland, July 1945.* (USN-NARS)

Fig. 29 *An F6F-5 lands on* **San Jacinto** *off Okinawa, March 1945. Of necessity, the Hellcats that had just landed are parked forward. Should a bolter miss all the wires, only three crash barriers stood to prevent disaster.* (USN-NARS)

was a popular variant as it retained all characteristics of the standard fighter. Because of its usefulness as a tactical reconaissance aircraft, F6F-5Ps lasted longer in the postwar Navy than most other Hellcats.

Grumman did make one attempt to significantly upgrade the Hellcat. A pair of F6F-5 airframes (BuNos 70188 & 70913) were fitted with 2100hp R-2800-18Ws and four-bladed props. The first of the two XF6F-6s flew on 6 July 1944, easily achieving a top speed of 417mph (671km/hr). The Navy, however, had finally pronounced itself pleased with the Vought Corsair and was concurrently testing the F4U-4 which could reach 440mph (708km/hr). Although Hellcat production continued for several months after war's end, the decision had been made in favour of the Corsair (and the F8F Bearcat) and further Hellcat development was abandoned.

Hellcats disappeared from the fleet after the war with a speed that belied their importance in the victory. Replaced on fleet carriers almost immediately, they did not last too much longer in land-based squadrons and were soon relegated to training or reserve duties. One further Hellcat variant was to see important, if somewhat humiliating, duty, the F6F-3K/5K radio-controlled drones. ''Ks'' were used for a number of important missions where human pilots could not or should not go. They were flown through the radioactive clouds of the postwar A-bomb tests and, laden with bombs, as guided missiles against exceptionally well guarded targets during the Korean War. Probably the most famous of those missions was against the railroad bridges at Hungnam in August 1952.

It is perhaps a bit unfair that Corsairs, based on an older design, should have still been flying off the fleet's carriers when Hellcats were being used as primitive cruise missiles or being relegated to the smelter. Still, the big fighter from the Iron Works need never be ashamed of its record. Hellcats accounted for over 75% of Japanese losses to US Navy fighters in WW2. They bore the brunt of Japan's best blows with ease. Perhaps therein lies the cause of the Hellcats' lack of glamour in the eyes of history. They made it look to easy.

Fig. 30 *'Butch' was an F6F-5N off* **Block Island.** *At this time, March 1945,* **Block Island** *was one of four escort carriers with an all-Marine air group, hence the 'M' in the tail marking.* (USMC)

Fig. 31 *Seen seconds before it burst into flames, this F6F-5 of* Lexington's *VF-20 demonstrates the risks of landing with a full drop tank, 25 February 1945. The pilot, Ens. A. R. Ives, caught the barrier, which ruptured his belly tank and spilled avgas under his Hellcat. Add smoking brakes and a fire was the inevitable result. As usual in these circumstances, Ives walked away unscathed. '23' was pitched over the side.* (USN/NARS)

Fig. 32 *A pair of VF-85 F6F-5s off* Shangri La *show off that carrier's 'G'-symbol, the letter 'Z', 17 August 1945. The one- or two-letter code introduced in July 1945 finally solved the problem of air group identification that had plagued the fleet since mid-1944.* (USN/NARS)

SPECIFICATIONS

XF6F-1

Dimensions: length, 33ft 7in (10236mm); span, 42ft 10in (13056mm); wing area, 334sq ft (31sq m).
Weights: gross weight, 11,630lb (5276kg); empty weight, 8480lb (3846kg).
Performance: max speed at 17,500ft (5334m), 375mph (604km/hr); rate of climb, 2350ft/min (716m/min); range, 1500 miles (2414km); ceiling, 35,500ft (10760m).
Powerplant: Wright R-2600-16 of 1600hp takeoff power.
Armament: 6×.50 (12.7mm) machine guns.

F6F-3

Dimensions: length, 33ft 7in (10236mm); span, 42ft 10in (13056mm); wing area, 334sq ft (31sq m).
Weights: gross weight, 13,221lb (5997kg); empty weight, 9025lb (4094kg).
Performance: max speed at 17,500ft (5334m), 376mph (605km/hr); rate of climb, 3100ft/min (945m/min); range, 1850 miles (2977km); ceiling, 38,400ft (11704m).
Powerplant: Pratt & Whitney R-2800-10 of 2000hp takeoff power.
Armament: 6×.50 (12.7mm) machine guns.

F6F-5

Dimensions: length, 33ft 7in (10236mm); span, 42ft 10in (13056mm); wing area, 334sq ft (31sq m).
Weights: gross weight, 12,598lb (5714kg); empty weight, 9060lb (4110kg).
Performance: max speed at 23,000ft, (7010m), 380mph (612km/hr); rate of climb, 3150ft/min (954m/min); range, 1900 miles (3058km); ceiling, 38,800ft (11826m).
Powerplant: Pratt & Whitney R-2800-10W of 2000hp takeoff power.
Armament: 6×.50 (12.7mm) machine guns or 2×20mm cannon.

VOUGHT F4U CORSAIR

Fig. 1 *A flight of four F4U-5s pass over the Wright Memorial, Kittyhawk, sometime between the wars. Markings were in a continual state of flux during this period and the diversity seen here (three with squadron insignia; two with underlined code) is typical.* (Vought)

Fig. 2 *The 13th production Corsair (BuNo 02169) sits in front of Vought's Bridgeport, CT, plant after completing a test flight. Most of the first production examples were used in the test programme aimed at correcting the minor lateral instability. While the problem was not great, it eventually took over 100 design changes to totally eliminate. Only the earliest Corsairs had the totally flat-topped sliding canopy.* (Vought)

When the US Navy's Bureau of Aeronautics (BuAer) issued the specifications for a new carrier interceptor in February 1938, they called for performance better than that of any contemporary warplane. The demand for a top speed well in excess of 350mph (563km/hr) at over 20,000ft (6096m), combined with the slow speed handling necessary for carrier landings, required an extension of the state-of-the-art in aircraft design. Such advances take time, but with the F2A and F4F prototypes in the air, BuAer obviously felt that the pace of events would allow the new fighter to be ready when needed. In this they were wrong. It would be 28 months after the US found itself unexpectedly at war that the fighter built in response to that 1938 specification, the Chance Vought F4U Corsair, would be considered ready for carrier duty. This delay in receiving complete operational clearance, however, did not prevent the new fighter from gaining a spectacular reputation as a potent fighting machine and the fearful respect of the enemy who dubbed it "Whistling Death". When the carriers finally got their hands on the Corsair, they could only conclude that it had been worth the wait.

In response to that specification, Chance Vought Aircraft Division of United Aircraft submitted a pair of designs to BuAer in April 1938. The V-166A proposal was to be powered by the existing Pratt & Whitney R-1830 Twin Wasp; the otherwise-identical V-166B was to have the proposed P&W XR-2800 Double Wasp 2000hp, 18-cylinder radial. Such was the Navy's desire to produce the ultimate carrier fighter that it turned down the "safer" Twin Wasp-powered version and on 11 June 1938 chose the V-166B. By February 1939,

Vought had a plywood mockup ready for BuAer's inspection.

The design that BuAer approved looked every bit as revolutionary as the specification that inspired it. To extract the maximum power from the huge new radial, Vought proposed hanging a three-bladed Hamilton-Standard propeller of 13ft 4in (4064mm) diameter in front of the Double Wasp. The very size of this propeller, by far the largest ever proposed for a single-engine aircraft, caused design problems. In order to keep the landing gear from getting too long and the ground angle reasonable while still allowing adequate ground clearance for the massive prop, Vought adopted the inverted gull-wing that became the Corsair's trademark. This design innovation brought two additional advantages. The pilot's downward vision was superior to that possible with a conventional wing and, because the wing joined the fuselage at nearly a right angle, the design could dispense with drag-inducing wing-to-fuselage fairings, further assisting performance. Vought incorporated other innovations into their new design. The XF4U-1, as the prototype was designated, was to be the first Navy aircraft to use spot-welding in its construction, saving weight, reducing drag and increasing strength, and the first to use direct exhaust injection to boost thrust. (At least one anachronistic feature was retained in the Corsair's design at the same time. The rear half of its folding outer wing sections was fabric covered, as were all control surfaces.)

The XF4U-1 (BuNo 01443) was ready for its first flight on 29 May 1940, powered by the still-experimental XR-2800-4, rated at 1850hp at takeoff and 1600hp at 15,000ft (4572m). The prototype carried a pair of .30 (7.62mm) Brownings in the cowling, firing through the propeller arc, and a single .50 (12.7mm) machine gun in each wing. Because the original specification envisioned bomber-interception as the new fighter's primary role, the prototype included a novel feature. In each outboard wing section was space for ten 5.2lb (2.4kg) fragmentation bombs designed to break up bomber formations. This idea was not unique to America but seems to have occurred to most other major air powers at about the same time. Germany and Japan both developed similar systems to the point of operational testing. Both found it totally ineffective and dropped it almost immediately. BuAer had the intelligence (or luck) to foresee that the system would be unworkable and deleted that feature from all future Corsairs.

From that initial flight, the Navy knew that it had a thoroughbred on its hands, though one that still had to be "broken'. Most of the initial problems seemed to stem from the experimental powerplant, which showed a nasty tendency to overheat and occasionally quit in midair. Airframe-related problems, mainly some lateral instability and aileron stiffness, seemed minor and easy to solve. Before there had been time to dispell this illusion, the prototype crashed on its fifth flight, on 12 July 1940, when caught in a thunderstorm while low on fuel. It took three months to rebuild the XF4U-1, which resumed test flying in October, now powered by a preproduction R-2800-8 of 2000hp takeoff power. BuAer was eager to let its own pilots try out the new fighter and ordered the immediate transfer of the prototype to NAS Anacostia for evaluation. Enroute, the XF4U-1 averaged 404mph (650km/hr) during one leg of the trip, making it the first US fighter to be able to sustain speeds in excess of 400mph (644km/hr).

To say that the Navy was impressed by its new bird would be an understatement. Yet it was not so impressed that it did not produce, after eight months of flight testing, a considerable list of corrections and changes to be introduced in the first production model. Among other changes, BuAer demanded an increase in aileron area in an effort to reduce stick forces in banks and rolls. More major changes resulted from reports of RAF experiences in the Battle of Britain. The RAF found that rifle-calibre .30 (7.62mm) weapons were largely ineffective in bringing down enemy aircraft. As a result, BuAer ordered the deletion of the Corsair's cowl-mounted .30s and the increase in wing-mounted .50s from two to six. This seemingly simple change was to have a serious effect on the fighter's design. In order to make room for three machine guns and ammunition in each wing, Vought was forced to relocate most of the fuel that had previously been stored in unprotected wing leading edge tanks into a single self-sealing tank in the fuselage. Such a large volume of fuel (237gal) (897ltr) in the fuselage would cause serious trim problems as it was used unless it was positioned at the aircraft's centre of gravity, above the wing. Placing a large fuel tank behind the firewall forced the aft relocation of the cockpit by some 32in (813mm). Despite the major nature of these changes, the Navy was confident that any problems could be rapidly solved and signed a contract for 584 F4U-1s on 30 June 1941, with deliveries to begin in February 1942. Now convinced that American involvement in the World War was inevitable, the Navy took steps to ensure that the new fighter would be available in unprecedented numbers. Soon after Vought received its first F4U contract, BuAer also ordered Brewster and Goodyear to begin tooling up for Corsair production (F3A-1 and FG-1 respectively) because they correctly predicted that no one manufacturing centre would be able to supply the quantities of Corsairs that would be needed. Nevertheless, it is doubtful that even the most

Fig. 3 *A flight of very early F4U-1s, probably August 1942. While these have the bulged canopy panel with rear-view mirror, they also have the cutouts on each side of the spine behind the pilot, characteristics of only the first hundred or so. The camouflage is unusual. It is either sea grey and white, in which case it is very non-standard, or it is a very early example of the Atlantic gull grey and white scheme.* (Vought)

Fig. 4 *An F4U-1 (BuNo 17450) in the Solomons, in late 1943. This is almost certainly a VMF-214 'Black Sheep' bird, meaning that the site is probably Vella Lavella. The national insignia had a red surround which has been removed and never replaced with blue, leaving the surroundless star and bar that characterised many Marine aircraft in the South Pacific at this time. Note that this aircraft had the rear-vision cutouts which have been plated over.* (Vought)

farsighted Navy planner could have guessed that F4U-1 production (including all ''-1'' variants) would reach 5,559, nor that over 12,000 Corsairs would be built before production finally ceased 12 years later.

Because of the extensive redesign demanded by BuAer, the first production F4U-1 (BuNo 02153) did not fly until 25 June 1942 and was not turned over to the Navy until early August. Powered by the production-standard R-2800-8 Double Wasp of 2000hp takeoff power, the F4U-1 could reach 417mph (671km/hr) at 20,000ft (6096m), climb at an initial rate of 3,120ft/min (951m/min) and had a service ceiling of 37,000ft (11277m). Almost unique among US fighters whose design origins stemmed from the pre-war period, fully-equipped production Corsairs were faster than the prototype. Again BuAer expressed itself pleased with its new fighter, until carquals began in August. Then the effects of the Corsair's redesign, which had seriously degraded slow-speed handling, suddenly came to the fore. The production Corsair was found to have poor forward vision when in the landing pattern, a direct consequence of the aft relocation of the cockpit. (That long nose was the inspiration for the Corsair's most enduring, if not endearing, nickname. It would be henceforce and forever ''Hognose''—also, alternatively, ''Hose Nose'', ''U-Bird'' or ''Ensign Eliminator''.)

The problems caused by that long nose proved difficult to solve because they interrelated with other handling deficiencies. If the pilot tried lowering the nose to get better vision, he gained speed too rapidly. If he kept the nose up, he was left with a very limited view of the carrier deck. A low cockpit canopy only made the problem worse by severely restricting a pilot's ability to raise his head to see over the nose. Visibility was frequently further hampered by chronic fluid leakage from the hydraulically-operated cowl flaps. But these problems were minor in comparison to the Corsair's stall characteristics. The F4U-1 stalled with little warning by suddenly dropping its left wing. Attempting to recover from a stall by suddenly increasing power was an invitation to further disaster. The torque generated by suddenly opening the throttle was often enough to flip a Corsair completely over. And even if a pilot managed to avoid a stall and bring his Corsair onboard, his problems were not over. If he missed his wire, he had little chance to recover because the Corsair's landing gear proved to be overly soft, leading to excessive bounce. An inexperienced pilot found it difficult not to overcorrect, increasing each bounce until he ended up in the barrier, or worse.

Suddenly, BuAer had a problem. Corsair production was well underway, but its fighter would be unsuitable for carrier ops until some major changes were made. In the meantime, they did what they always did when they had aircraft that they could not think of anything else to do with . . . they gave them to the Marines. For once in that long, often unfortunate, relationship the Marine Corps did not mind playing second fiddle. They ended up being the first service to take the new Corsair into action. VMF-124 formed on the first batch of F4U-1s at Camp Kearney, CA, in September 1942 and reached Guadalcanal in February 1943.

Fig. 5 *This view of a new F4U-1A on Vought's Bridgeport assembly line shows some of the clever engineering which made the Corsair so successful. Radial engines were tough and lightweight but had that great frontal area with the ensuing drag. The close cowling kept drag to a minimum but also allowed marginal cooling. Vought's design placed oil coolers and supercharger intakes in the wingroots, keeping extra protrusions to a minimum. There was so little extra cooling available, though, that later variants with more powerful, higher altitude engines needed extra airscoops.* (Vought)

Fig. 6 *Waist-deep in Corsair, a groundcrewman stands in the main fuel tank of this Marine F4U-1A (BuNo 17818), Solomons, 1944. Major repairs are going on; the inboard flap on the near side has been removed. The rubber body of the self-sealing tank can be seen.* (Vought)

Fig. 7 *The use of Corsairs as fighter-bombers was inevitable. What was surprising was just how good an attacker the F4U turned out to be. In late 1943, in response to some early experiments by VMF-222 and VF-17, Vought sent a team of experts led by Charles Lindburgh to the Pacific to check-out the Corsair as a bomber. With their endorsement, a standard centreline bomb rack was designed by Brewster and bomb pylons were added to the design of the forthcoming F4U-1D. A Marine '-1A' is seen late war with Brewster Rack and field-fitted rocket stubs.* (Vought)

Its combat debut was something less than spectacular. In a combined operation with USAAF Liberators, P-38s and P-40s on 14 February, VMF-124's Corsairs were jumped by over 50 Zekes who hit from above, dived through the American formation and departed, having downed 10 US aircraft, including two Corsairs, for the loss of only four of their own.

The young Marines can perhaps be excused for their poor showing the first time out. In the rush to get the Corsair into combat, VMF-124's pilots averaged only about 20 hours in their new mounts, not nearly enough time to transition from Buffalos or Wildcats into the hottest thing in the air. The Marines were fast learners, though, and the Corsair was rarely again at the short end of the score. VMF-124 rapidly evolved the tactics that would become the Corsair's standard mode of attack. Taking advantage of the F4U's superior climb and high-altitude performance, the Marines quickly learned to do unto the Zero as it had first done unto them. The basic tactic was to gain an altitude advantage and dive through enemy formations, using the six .50s along the way to cause maximum damage, avoiding enemy attack by means of superior speed, quickly disengaging and climbing back on top to start it all over again. The F4U-1 was slightly less manoeuvrable than the Hellcat and could not dogfight with a Zeke, particularly at lower altitudes. Unlike a Hellcat, however, the Corsair could outrun a Zeke at all altitudes, climbing as well as diving,

and thus had little to fear from such an engagement. The Marines found that they had no need of the "Thach Weave" manoeuvre that the Navy had devised to protect its Wildcats from attack and was used regularly by Hellcats in defensive situations. The Corsair simply ran away from any trouble it could not handle.

Needless to say, this was the beginning of the Marine Corps' love affair with the "Hognose" that was to last for more than a dozen years. Tales of the Corsair's great abilities soon spread as VMF-124 ran up its score and other F4U-1-equipped VMFs joined the fight. The first Corsair ace was Lt Kenneth A. Walsh of the 124 squadron, who reached six by shooting down three bandits over Henderson Field on 13 May 1943. The greatest of the Marine Corsair aces was undoubtedly Lt Robert Hanson of VMF-215, who achieved an incredible total of 20 victories in one span of 17 days. Joining VMF-215 on 6 October 1943, Hanson gained his first victory on 1 November. He already was an ace with five victories when his record-breaking string began over Rabaul on 14 January 1944. He got five that day, four each on the 24th and 30th, three on the 17th and 26th and one on the 15th, bring his total to 25. VMF-215 raided Rabaul again on 3 February but found it clouded over. On the way back to Torokina, Bougainville, Hanson dropped down to strafe a Japanese flak position on New Ireland, took a hit and cartwheeled into the sea. The most famous Corsair ace, and the leading Marine ace of the war (counting six victories gained with the AVG in China) was Major Gregory Boyington, CO of VMF-214, the legendary "Black Sheep".

F4U-1 production ended with the 758th example, being replaced on the line by the revised F4U-1A. This version incorporated the changes Vought believed would solve the Corsair's carrier landing problems. While the cockpit could not be moved again, pilot's vision was significantly improved by raising the seat by 7in (178mm) and providing a bulged canopy. Similarly, the stall problem could not be completely solved but it was brought under control by the addition of a "stall strip" to the starboard wing. This was a 6in (152mm) triangular strip added to the wing's leading edge just outboard of the guns. It served to disrupt airflow over that wing sufficiently so that both wings now stalled at the same time, taking much of the terror out of a stall on approach. Taxiing vision was improved by lengthening the tailwheel struts. Finally, power was increased by the adoption of water injection. The R-2800-8W, first fitted to the 862nd Corsair, boosted takeoff power to 2,250hp.

The F4U-1A went a long way towards answering the Navy's objections to the Corsair as a carrier fighter but BuAer continued to deny carrier clearance to the Corsair day fighter. There was more than a little hypocrisy in this refusal because by the time the ban was finally lifted, Corsair night fighters had been operated off fleet carriers in combat for at least two months and day fighters had been staging off carrier decks for nearly a year. VF(N)-101 took its F4U-2s onboard *Intrepid* and *Enterprise* before the Truk raids of February 1944. The 32 "official" F4U-2s were stock F4U-1s (low seat and all) that had been modified by the Naval Aircraft Factory to become the Navy's first night fighter. (Two additional Corsairs were field-modified by Marine units in the South Pacific and operated by VMF(N)-532.) The modification included the mounting of an AN/APS-6 radar pod on the starboard wing leading edge and the removal of the outboard .50 on that side to compensate. Cockpit layout was altered by the addition of the big radar screen and provision for radio altimeter and increased-range communication equipment. The XF4U-2 (BuNo 02153) was the initial production F4U-1, modified in early 1943. The pace of modification was slow because of a limited supply of radars and delivery to the fleet lagged because tactics had to be developed and operational procedures tested. Nevertheless, the F4U-2s became the first carrier-based night fighters when they deployed in early 1944. (The first night fighter Hellcats arrived only a few weeks later. The Hellcat was generally preferred as a night fighter because of its more docile slow speed characteristics.) It is more than a little absurd that an aircraft considered unsafe for daylight carrier operations should be assigned to much riskier night duty but that is exactly what happened. It must have chagrined more than a few "armchair admirals" when field reports showed the Corsair

Fig. 8 *A flight of Marine F4U-1As, each with a 500lb (227kg) bomb on its Brewster Rack, taxies out prior to a strike, sometime in 1944. Time must have been short between strikes, or the groundcrew lazy, because 272's gunports have not been taped.* (Vought)

Fig. 9 *The F4U-1C was basically a '-1D' with its .50s replaced by four 20mm cannons. The slower rate of fire of the cannons made the '-1C' less versatile in air combat but greatly increased its effectiveness in strafing runs. Some pilots, particularly night fighters, liked the fact that fewer hits (therefore less time on target) were necessary to bring down a target.* (Vought)

no more accident-prone than the Hellcat in night operations. (The technique evolved by these early Corsair "jocks" for bringing a "Hognose" safely onboard rapidly became the standard. It required keeping airspeed up above stall, absolute faith in the LSO—a good idea under any circumstances—and a late, sweeping turn off the downwind leg with a minimal straight-way at the end. This allowed the LSO to be kept in sight throughout the entire approach and usually resulted in a good trap.)

With F4U-1As coming off three assembly lines by mid-1943, the Navy finally decided the time had come to deploy a Corsair squadron of its own, though still refusing to sanction carrier operations. Accordingly, VF-17 was formed on New Year's Day 1943 and worked up on F4U-1s before it got its "-1As" and deployed to New Georgia in September. If the Navy had any continuing doubts about the combat effectiveness of the Corsair, the "Jolly Rogers" of VF-17 certainly

dispelled them because they proceeded to write a combat record probably unequalled before or since. In 76 days, VF-17 shot down 127 enemy aircraft (including 60 in one five-day stretch), sank five ships and maintained a victory ratio of better than 8 to 1. During that period, no fewer than 12 Jolly Rogers became aces. The most successful of them was Ens Ira Kepford who claimed 17 victories before being rotated back to the States. At that time Ira Kepford was the leading Navy ace.

VF-17, among its many accomplishments, also added its contribution to convincing BuAer that Corsairs were carrier-capable. Flying from New Georgia on 8 November 1943, VF-17 took up CAP duties over *Essex* and *Bunker Hill* (TG 50.3) while the latter launched a strike on Rabaul. The Japanese response was unexpectedly strong and VF-17 was soon engaged in heavy combat over the fleet. With fuel running low, the Corsairs could either break for home, leaving the carriers exposed, or break all the rules, land onboard, rearm,

Fig. 10. Above *The usefulness of the Corsair as a fighter-bomber led to the F4U-1D, which had three external stores positions, two pylons and the centreline. This view of the 19th '-1D' (BuNo 50378) at Bridgeport shows a typical load, a pair of 1000lb (454kg) bombs. Early F4U-1Ds retained the 'braced' canopy of the '-1A'.* (Vought)

Fig. 11 Below *Early in the F4U-1D production run, successful experiments with 5" HVARs led to the adoption of four zero-length launchers under each wing outer panel. One of the test airframes is seen here with dummy rockets, early 1944.* (Vought)

Fig. 12 *By the time of the invasion of Iwo Jima, February 1945, Corsairs finally began to operate 'officially' off carrier decks. Many carriers involved in that action adopted a yellow cowl ring as a temporary operational marking. These later-production F4U-1Ds of VF-84 on* Bunker Hill *carry that marking with a patch of glossy sea blue left on each side of the cowling so that the aircraft number did not have to be repainted. Note that the four Hellcat night fighters also carry that marking but the six Helldivers do not.* (Vought)

refuel and rejoin the battle. Needless to say, VF-17 became the first unit to fly combat ops off a carrier. After that first occasion, Corsair operations became more common on US carriers, although the official ban still made it impossible to station Corsairs onboard. (The honour of flying the first ''official'' combat off a carrier fell to the Royal Navy's No. 1834 Squadron which, on 3 April 1944, flew Corsairs off HMS *Victorious* during Operation Tungsten, one of the many raids on *Tirpitz*.)

It was the acceptance of the F4U-1D (combined with the fact that they were doing it anyway) which finally forced BuAer to lift its ban on carrier duty by the Corsair on 22 April 1944. F4U-1A production ended at this time after 2066 had been built. The main difference between the ''-1A'' and ''-1D'' was the adoption of longer-stroke, stiffer oleo struts which brought the Corsair's bouncing problem under control. The only other visible difference was the addition of twin pylons for bombs or fuel tanks under the wing centre section, augmenting the centreline station. The additional weight

that could be carried on the new pylons would open up a whole new field for the Corsair, a field in which it would excel, that of fighter-bomber. A number of other changes were made during the early phases of the ''-1D'' production run. These included the adoption of a frameless sliding canopy, the removal of the antenna to behind the cockpit and the fitting of four zero-length rocket launchers under each wing. The performance of the ''-1D'' in unladen conditions was virtually identical to the ''-1As'', it being powered by the same R-2800-8W. In all 3862 F4U-1Ds would be built by Vought and Goodyear (Brewster having been dropped from the programme for gross inefficiency).

The Corsair fighter-bomber had a very enthusiastic supporter. In late 1943, Vought had asked Charles A. Lindbergh to make a tour of frontlines in the Pacific and report on early experiments. He was under specific instructions to observe only, but once at the front he could not resist making some very realistic test flights over Japanese-held islands. On one occasion, he flew from

Roi (Kwajalein) to Wotke, a distance of about 200nm (370km), carrying a 2000lb (907kg) bomb on the centre-line and a 1000lb (454kg) bomb on each pylon, where he "tested" a Japanese AA position to destruction. (A fully-loaded B-17, in comparison, could carry just double that load, 8000lb (3630kg).)

Once official approval had been granted, the fleet demanded Corsair squadrons as soon as possible. Still, it would be early 1945 before the first Corsair-equipped VFs were ready. Not unexpectedly, the Marines got there first. VMF-124 and VMF-213 reported aboard *Essex* on 28 December 1944, the US Navy's first ship-board Corsair squadrons. By the time of the Okinawa Campaign in March 1945, there were 10 F4U-1D-equipped squadrons with the fleet: 4 VMFs, 3 VBFs and 3 VFs (VF-10 on *Intrepid*, VF-5 on *Franklin*, VF-84 on *Bunker Hill*). From that point on, the changeover from Hellcat to Corsair was rapid. By war's end, the Hellcat had effectively been phased out in favour of the F4U-1D.

Two other F4U-1 variants were given official designations. F4U-1B was the name loosely and inconsistently applied to the F4U-1s and F4U-1As supplied by Lend

Lease to the RN. The F4U-1Cs were "-1Ds" with the three .50 (12.7mm) machine guns in each wing replaced by two M-2 20mm cannon, specifically to exploit the ground attack potential of the Corsair. Two hundred were built.

In the F4U-1D, the Corsair can finally be said to have reached maturity. The Corsair's speed and power were finally controlled to the extent that carrier operations were no more dangerous in the F4U than in any of its contemporaries, albeit a bit more tricky. In the Corsair, the Navy had arguably the best all-round fighter in the world. Of this they were convinced. Several times in its career, BuAer flew its Corsair against the best captured enemy fighters and against the best USAAF had to offer, specifically the P-51 Mustang. Not only did the Corsair outfly every enemy aircraft but it consistently equalled or outperformed the Mustang in nearly all pertinent categories. Specifically, it could match the Mustang stride-for-stride at most altitudes, was very nearly as manoeuvrable, could absorb more punishment and could outcarry it at all ranges. There was no doubt at BuAer that in the F4U-1D, the Navy had, quality-for-quality, the best single fighting machine in the air.

Fig. 13 *By the time of the Okinawa invasion, April 1945, the yellow ring had disappeared. Here a deckload of* Bunker Hill's *F4U-1Ds is loaded and ready to launch in support of the troops. Each has a single external tank and eight 5" (127mm) HVARs, which were found to be more effective and easier to aim than bombs. The carrier-based, and later land-based Marine, Corsair proved so effective in close support that the Marines gratefully called it the 'Angel of Okinawa'.* (Vought)

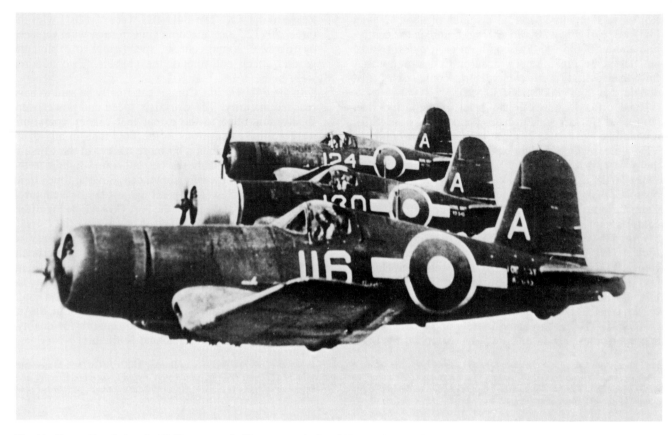

Fig. 14. Above *Even before the US Navy operated off its carriers, the Royal Navy understood that its great qualities outweighed any faults and adopted the Corsair as its standard naval fighter. Here a flight of three Corsair IVs (FG-1Ds) off HMS* **Vengeance** *in SEAC markings are seen in 1945.* (Vought)

Fig. 15. Below *A Royal Navy Corsair IV prepares to launch off* **Shangri La** *off Japan, 21 July 1945. KD244 was a Goodyear-built FG-1A (ex-BuNo 14675).* (USN-NARS)

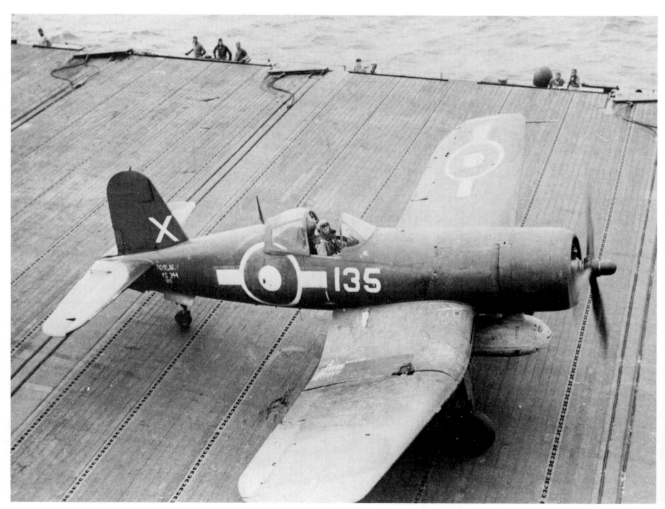

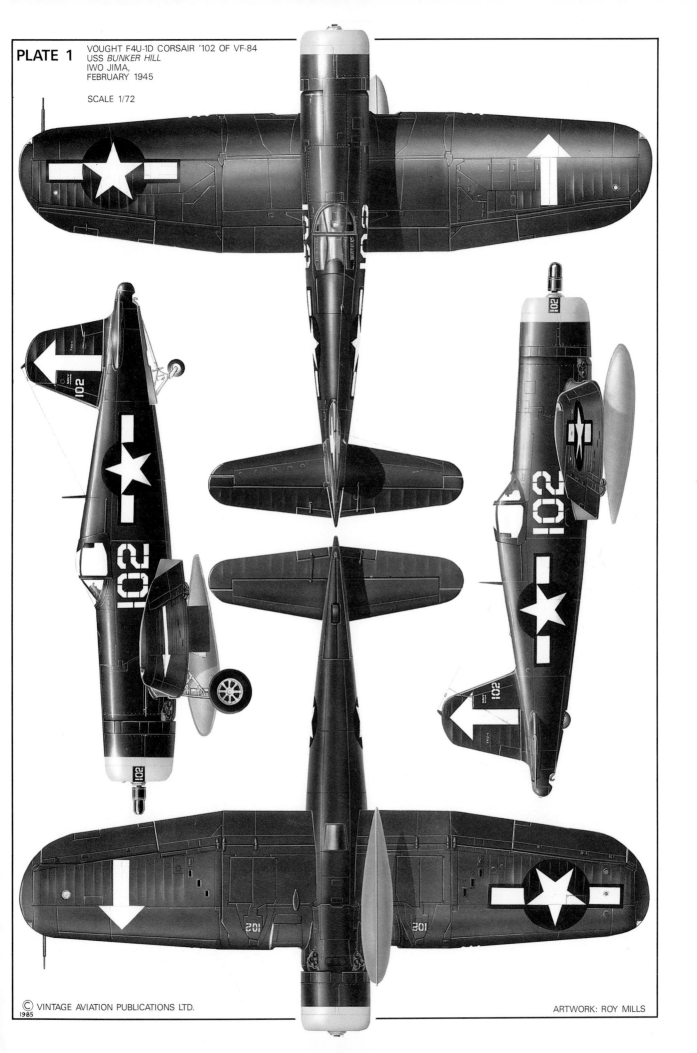

PLATE 1

VOUGHT F4U-1D CORSAIR '102 OF VF-84
USS *BUNKER HILL*
IWO JIMA,
FEBRUARY 1945

SCALE 1/72

© VINTAGE AVIATION PUBLICATIONS LTD.
1985

ARTWORK: ROY MILLS

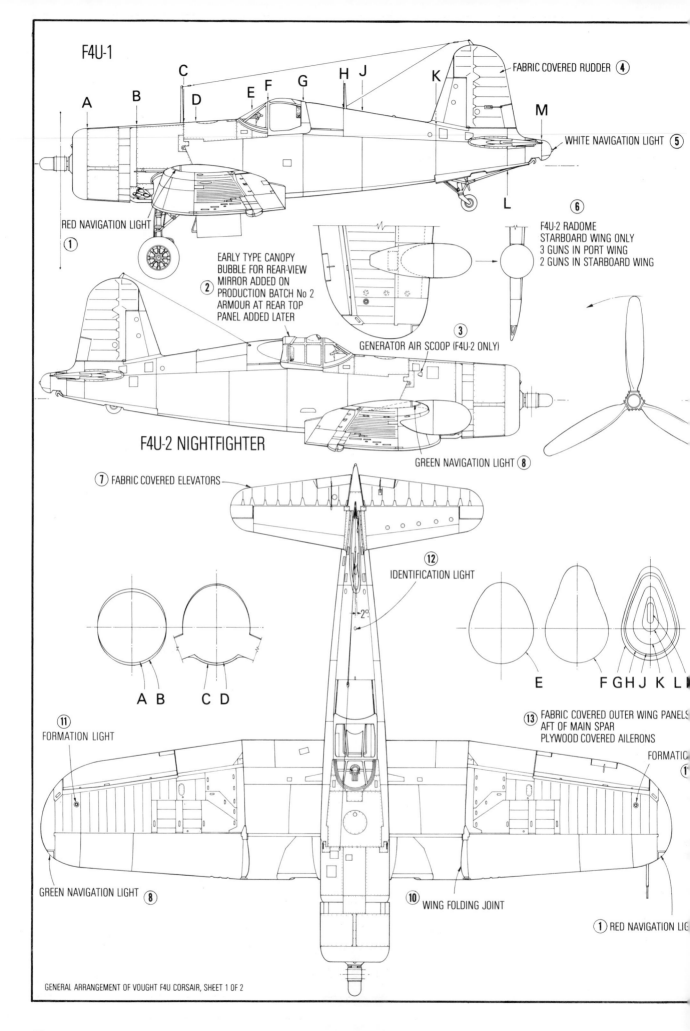

F4U-1

RED NAVIGATION LIGHT ①

FABRIC COVERED RUDDER ④

WHITE NAVIGATION LIGHT ⑤

EARLY TYPE CANOPY
BUBBLE FOR REAR-VIEW
MIRROR ADDED ON
② PRODUCTION BATCH No 2
ARMOUR AT REAR TOP
PANEL ADDED LATER

③ GENERATOR AIR SCOOP (F4U-2 ONLY)

⑥
F4U-2 RADOME
STARBOARD WING ONLY
3 GUNS IN PORT WING
2 GUNS IN STARBOARD WING

F4U-2 NIGHTFIGHTER

GREEN NAVIGATION LIGHT ⑧

⑦ FABRIC COVERED ELEVATORS

⑫ IDENTIFICATION LIGHT

⑪ FORMATION LIGHT

A B   C D

E   F G H J K L

⑬ FABRIC COVERED OUTER WING PANELS
AFT OF MAIN SPAR
PLYWOOD COVERED AILERONS

FORMATIO

GREEN NAVIGATION LIGHT ⑧

⑩ WING FOLDING JOINT

① RED NAVIGATION LIG

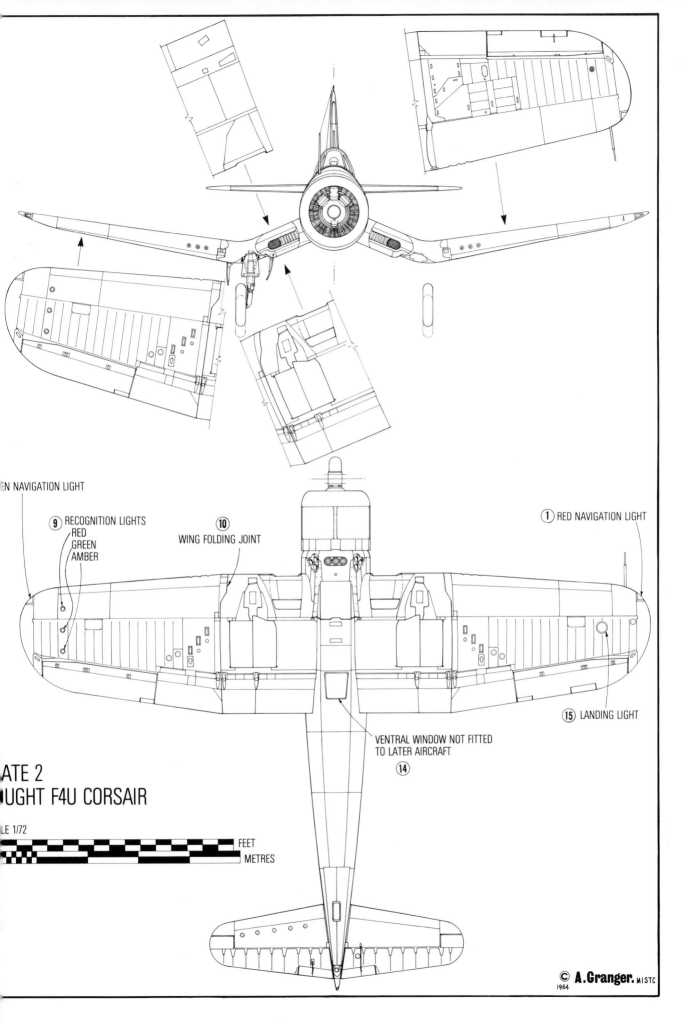

EN NAVIGATION LIGHT

(9) RECOGNITION LIGHTS
RED
GREEN
AMBER

(10) WING FOLDING JOINT

(1) RED NAVIGATION LIGHT

(15) LANDING LIGHT

VENTRAL WINDOW NOT FITTED
TO LATER AIRCRAFT
(14)

ATE 2
UGHT F4U CORSAIR

LE 1/72

FEET
METRES

© A.Granger. MISTC
1984

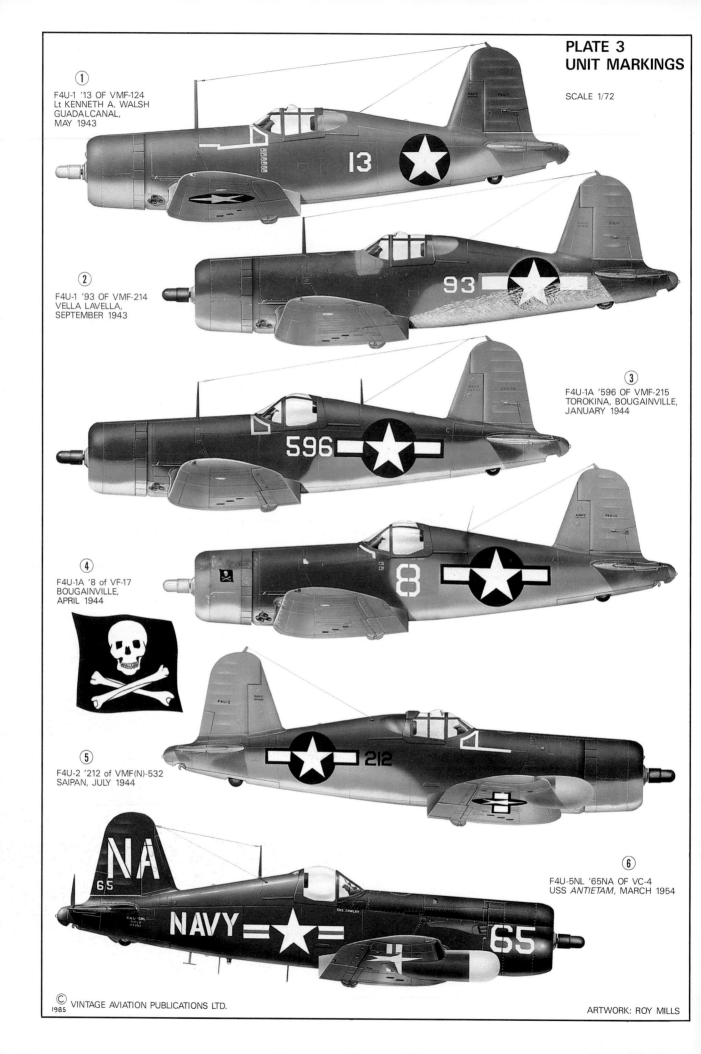

PLATE 3
UNIT MARKINGS

SCALE 1/72

① F4U-1 '13 OF VMF-124
Lt KENNETH A. WALSH
GUADALCANAL,
MAY 1943

② F4U-1 '93 OF VMF-214
VELLA LAVELLA,
SEPTEMBER 1943

③ F4U-1A '596 OF VMF-215
TOROKINA, BOUGAINVILLE,
JANUARY 1944

④ F4U-1A '8 of VF-17
BOUGAINVILLE,
APRIL 1944

⑤ F4U-2 '212 of VMF(N)-532
SAIPAN, JULY 1944

⑥ F4U-5NL '65NA OF VC-4
USS ANTIETAM, MARCH 1954

ARTWORK: ROY MILLS

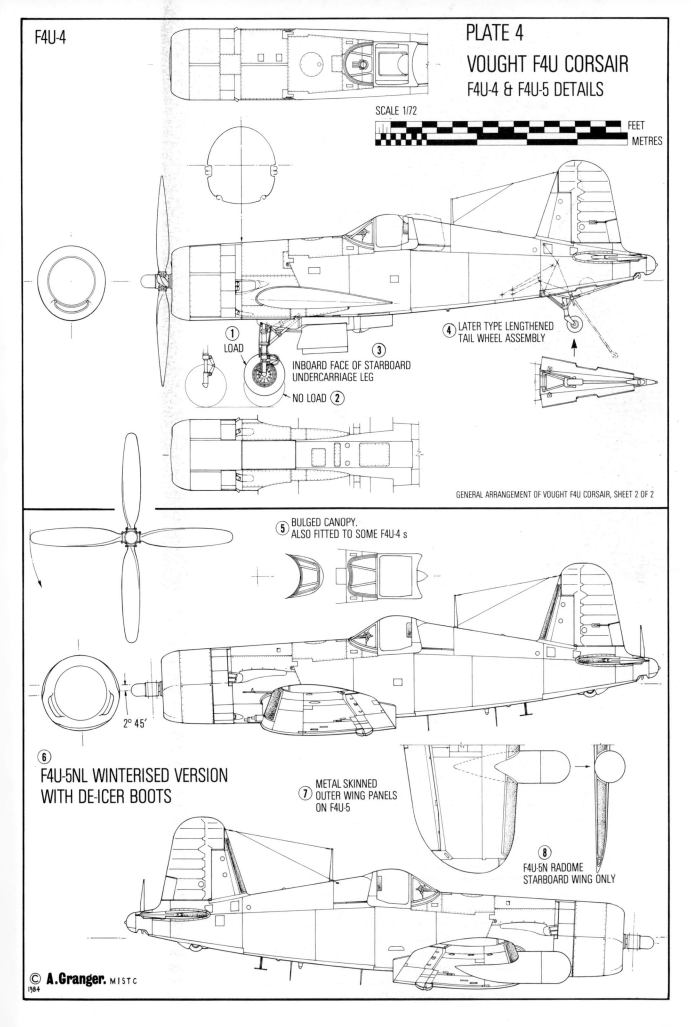

F4U-4

PLATE 4
VOUGHT F4U CORSAIR
F4U-4 & F4U-5 DETAILS

SCALE 1/72

FEET
METRES

① LOAD
INBOARD FACE OF STARBOARD
③ UNDERCARRIAGE LEG
NO LOAD ②

④ LATER TYPE LENGTHENED
TAIL WHEEL ASSEMBLY

GENERAL ARRANGEMENT OF VOUGHT F4U CORSAIR, SHEET 2 OF 2

⑤ BULGED CANOPY.
ALSO FITTED TO SOME F4U-4 s

2° 45'

⑥
F4U-5NL WINTERISED VERSION
WITH DE-ICER BOOTS

METAL SKINNED
⑦ OUTER WING PANELS
ON F4U-5

⑧
F4U-5N RADOME
STARBOARD WING ONLY

© A. Granger. M I S T C
1984

Fig. 16. Above *F4U-1Ds served in reserve units for many years after the war. To celebrate an event long since forgotten, at least five reserve squadrons have mustered, making for an impressive display of Corsair power, 9 August 1948. The tailcodes identify the homebase of these squadrons: AF from Anacostia(DC), CF from Columbus(OH), FF from Oakland(CA), HF from Miami(FL) and IF from Grosse Isle(MI). A three foot (914mm) wide orange band encircles the fuselage at the national insignia.* (Vought)

Fig. 17. Below *Corsair night fighters, F4U-2s modified from low-cockpit F4U-1s, operated off carriers well before the official ban was lifted. Three of the four F4U-2s of VF(N)-101 Det B can be seen on the deck of* **Intrepid**, *early 1944.* (Vought)

Fig. 18 *Marine F4U-2s of VMF(N)-532 flew off the escort carrier* **Windham Bay** *en route to Saipan, 12 July 1944. Because of the short deck, the Corsairs needed the full length to get airborne. As '205' starts its run, the next is spotted aft, two more have their wings extended, while four still have wings folded and braced. There is a tantalising glimpse of a unit insignia on the cowling of '208'.* (USN via Sullivan)

Fig. 19 *BuNo 17516 was an F4U-1A converted into one of the three XF4U-3s fitted with the experimental XR-2800-16(C) of 2000hp takeoff power. The need for additional intake area caused by the adoption of more powerful versions of the Double Wasp, which led to the extended chin of the '-4', has been solved here by a rather bulky ventral scoop, 1944.* (Vought)

Despite BuAer's obvious cause for satisfaction with the F4U-1D, there was no time for resting on laurels. When Pratt & Whitney proposed an improved Double Wasp in early 1944, the R-2800-18W of 2450hp takeoff power, BuAer immediately expressed an interest and ordered Vought to produce a pair of prototypes powered by the new engine. BuNos 49763 and 50301 were taken out of the F4U-1A sequence, fitted with a large chin scoop to supplement the wingroot airscoops and, curiously, designated as F4U-4Xs. The first flight was on 19 April 1944. With the new, more powerful Double Wasp driving a four-bladed, 13ft 2in (4013mm) diameter Hamilton Standard prop, the prototypes reached 451mph (726km/hr) at altitude and climbed at better than 4000ft/min (1219m/min). Pleased with the improved performance, the Navy ordered five purpose-built prototypes to test proposed changes in cockpit layout and to serve as pre-production test craft. The five XF4U-4s featured a redesigned cockpit with improved seating, somewhat increased rearward visibility because the metal overhang behind the pilot's head was removed and improved forward visibility because the armour glass was made integral with the windscreen. Production

examples followed as soon as the necessary changes could be made on the lines, the first being accepted by the Navy on 31 October 1944. The first ''-4''-equipped units began to deploy on fleet carriers in May 1945 and were able to participate in the final months of the war. (There had been three prototypes of a proposed ''-3'' Corsair, which was to have been powered by the experimental XR-2800-16(C). Because the engine proved to actually deliver only about 2000hp, less than the production R-2800-8W, the project was dropped and the XF4U-3s used for other purposes.)

2045 standard day fighter F4U-4s were produced before the end of the model run in August 1947. (Production pace slowed markedly at war's end. In fact, the Corsair was virtually unique in that production continued past VJ-Day.) 287 F4U-4Bs were ordered by the Royal Navy but cancelled as victory seemed assured. 300 F4U-4Cs were equipped with four 20mm cannon in an arrangement identical to the ''-1C's''. Many of these were later converted by NAF to F4U-4N standard by the addition of AN/APS-6 radar. Finally, 11 F4U-4Ps were completed with a single obliquely-mounted K-21 camera for tactical reconnaissance.

Fig. 20. Above *One of the '-3' prototypes (BuNo 49664) was further modified into a ground attack variant, the XF4U-3B, by the addition of extra armour and the re-arrangement of some internal systems, another idea whose time had not yet come.* (Vought)

Fig. 21. Below *Various ideas for up-powering and generally improving the basic Corsair were brought together in the two F4U-4Xs, the first of which (BuNo 49763, an ex-F4U-1A) is seen here in flight, 1944. The most obvious new features were the chin scoop and the four-bladed prop.* (Vought)

Fig. 22. Above *An F4U-1D of VMF-311 prepares to launch off* Breton *on 7 April 1945, off the coast of Okinawa. The squadron flew off to land bases that day, going into combat immediately in the ground support role. VMF-311's Hell's Belles were the first to take cannon-armed F4U-1C (note '327' to the left in this photo) into combat. They proved to be extremely popular with their Marine pilots.* (USN-NARS)

Fig. 23. Below *Among the first units engaged in Korea was VMF-214, the infamous 'Black Sheep' of such bawdy (largely undeserved) reputation. Here a cannon-armed '-214' F4U-4B prepares to launch against targets near Pusan during the desperate early days of the war. Note the full load of 5″ (127mm) HVARs. Besides the two cannons in each wing, '-4Bs' had a staggered arrangement of rocket stowage, USS* Sicily, *August 1950.* (Vought)

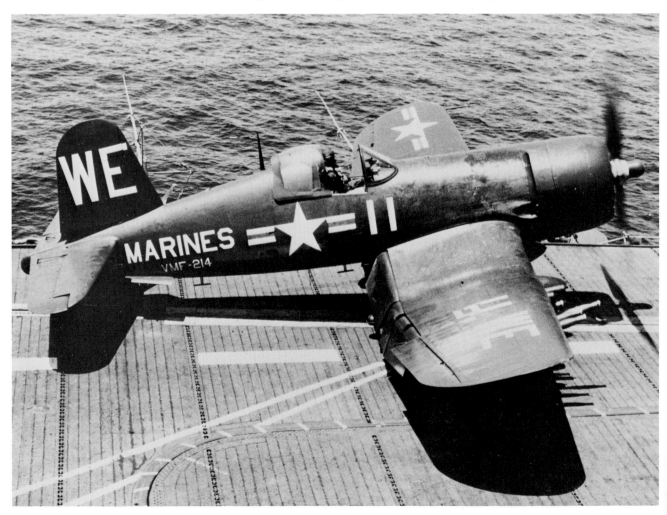

Fig. 24 *An F4U-5N is flight tested over NAS Dallas, where Vought relocated after WW2. The night fighter variant had an extra antenna behind the rudder as well as the AN/APS-19 radar, 1950.* (Vought)

Like its USAAF (later USAF) ''rival'', the P-51 Mustang, development of the Corsair did not cease at war's end. But while the continued development of the Mustang was anomalous (the lightweight P-51H and twin-engined F-82) and not totally successful, Corsair evolution was very much in line with previous development. The XF4U-5 was a straightforward ''-4'' follow-on, optimised for high-altitude performance, which first flew on 21 December 1945. Powered by the still more powerful R-2800-32WE with two-stage, variable-speed supercharger, giving 2450hp ''dry'' (i.e. without water injection), the prototype reached 462mph (744km/hr), nearly as fast as any production prop-driven fighter would ever go and easily faster than any other piston-powered carrier aircraft. (In comparison, the ultimate Grumman, the F8F Bearcat, had a top speed of 447mph (719km/hr).) A number of other changes were made from the F4U-4. The single chin scoop of that model became twin ''cheek'' scoops to further increase air intake at altitude. Springtabs were fitted to the ailerons, finally solving the Corsair's roll stiffness. Cannon armament became standard and electrical heating was in-

stalled in the ammo bays, again in response to conditions at extreme altitudes. Finally, the most outdated feature of the Corsair, the fabric-covered wing outer sections, were metal skinned in the ''-5''.

The F4U-5 was very much the ultimate Corsair. Even the F2G was no better. This latter was the result of a proposal by BuAer to Vought, which turned the project over to Goodyear, to try the 3000hp (3600hp with water injection) 4-row, 26 cylinder Pratt & Whitney R-4360-4 Wasp major in the Corsair airframe. The idea was to produce a Corsair optimised for low-altitude performance to help counter the kamikaze threat. The resulting XF2G-1 (BuNo 13471), which first flew in late 1944, was a brute of an aircraft, capable of reaching 400mph (644km/hr) at sea level and reaching 30,000ft (9144m) in just four minutes (7,500ft/min) (2286m/min) but not surprisingly slower than the F4U-4 at altitude (431mph (694km/hr) *v.* 451mph (726km/hr) at 16,000ft (4877m)). The Wasp Major was longer but had a smaller diameter than the Double Wasp which gave the F2G a unique forward end, a long narrow cowling stretching back to the wing leading edge, followed by a prominent

Fig. 25 & 26 *In response to the bitter weather found in Korea, Vought modified 101 of the '-5N' night fighters into winterised '-5NLs'. The only obvious external difference was the de-icer boots on all flight surfaces. Ens. Cawley's F4U-5NL is given a final check by the deckcrew before launching off* Antietam, March 1954. (Vought)

Fig. 27 *The last Corsair variant produced for US forces was the AU-1 intended for the Marines. Distinguishing features were the lack of cowling scoops, cannon armament, five rocket rails under each wing and extra blade antenna on the spine.* (Vought)

AN/APS-19A, and APS-6 derivative), 101 were winterised F4U-5NLs (with de-icer boots, the first fighter to be so equipped) specifically built to meet conditions in Korea, and 30 reconnaissance F4U-5Ps.

The war in Korea broke out on 25 June 1950, Corsairs (F4U-4s and F4U-5s) becoming involved almost immediately. The F4U was still very much first-line equipment on fleet carriers, jets being still in their infancy, particularly at sea. (Jets first entered the fleet in March 1948 and were increasing in range and reliability throughout this period, but the anticipated transition to all-jet CAGs had not taken place—and still has not! Jets had an obvious speed advantage in the interceptor role but lacked the range for long-range interdiction or air superiority missions and were of unproven survivability in the attack role. CAG-5, the first naval air unit engaged in Korea, had two VFs of F9F Panthers and two of Corsairs.) The Corsairs of VF-53 and -54 flew off *Valley Forge* against Pyongyang in early July 1950, the first US Navy strikes of this long, indecisive war. Other carriers soon joined *Valley Forge*. *Phillipine Sea* with VF-113 and -114, *Sicily* with VMF-214 (yes, the "Black Sheep") and *Badoeng Strait* with VMF-323 formed the Navy's initial deployment. As the war progressed, the names of the carriers and units changed but the Corsair was consistently in action throughout the conflict. In

dorsal airscoop. There were to have been two production versions, the land-based "-1" which lacked arresting gear and the carrier-based "-2" which retained all naval equipment. BuAer recognised the fact that the F2G, while obviously successful at its designed task, would be of limited usefulness once the war was over and dragged its feet on the project until the need for a low-altitude fighter ceased to exist. Along the way, 18 F2Gs, including "X" models, were completed. "Production" F2Gs incorporated a feature that many Navy pilots would have liked to have seen on standard Corsairs, a cut-down rear fuselage and true bubble canopy. At least one F2G-1D was built with a heightened tail which included an auxiliary rudder, further improving handling. Despite its many fine qualities, the F2G-series represented a "dead end" line of development (at least as seen from the perspective of 1945) and was never seriously pursued.

On the other hand, the F4U-5 represented very much the mainstream of Navy thinking and was accepted immediately. The end of the war eliminated any urgency in Corsair procurement, thus the first production "-5" was not delivered until April 1946. War's end also greatly reduced the demand for new aircraft leading to a total "-5" produciton of only 568. Of these, 223 were day fighters, 214 were radar-equipped F4U-5Ns (with

Fig. 28 *An AU-1 in flight over Dallas, 1952, before delivery to the Marines. The camouflage is absolutely textbook, overall glossy sea blue with dull black antiglare panel in front of the pilot. The two paints could often only be distinguished when new. The national insignia is only red and white, the background being the basic sea blue.* (Vought)

fact, more Corsair units were engaged at the end of the Korean Conflict than at any time during that war because Marine land-based night fighter and attack units flying Corsairs continued to proliferate. The only Corsair ace of the Korean War (also the only Navy ace, the only prop-driven ace and the only night fighter ace) was Lt Guy Bordelon who shot down five La-11s and Yak-18s during a short period in 1953, flying an F4U-5N (BuNo 124453) for VC-3 out of K-16 airfield. It is ironic that the Corsair, long dreaded because of its vicious slow-speed characteristics, achieved its final glory at speeds that often dropped to 90 knots (167km/hr).

One other Corsair version appeared in direct response to the needs of the Korean War, a version optimised for low altitudes like the F2G but created for totally different reasons. F4Us were being employed with success as ground attackers in Korea, but there were some, par-

ticularly Marines, who felt that a purpose-built version would do an even better job. Therefore, the Marines attempted to get Congressional approval for the procurement of an attack-dedicated Corsair. Here they ran into unexpected resistance. A number of legislators objected to spending money on what was now a 13-year-old aircraft, flatly refusing to fund another variant of the F4U. Nevertheless, these same men readily approved 111 AU-1s in late 1951, perhaps not aware that it was the Corsair that the Marines wanted.

The AU-1 looked a great deal like an early Corsair but was, in fact, basically an F4U-5 with the supercharger intakes removed. The R-2800-83W was boosted by a two-speed, manually-controlled, single-stage supercharger and was capable of delivering 2300hp for takeoff. Other visible changes included the addition of a fifth rocket rail under each wing. Internally, the oil coolers were moved from their vulnerable position in the

Fig. 29 *The last of the Corsairs was F4U-7 produced for the Aeronavale. The '-7' had a chin scoop like the '-4' but was armed like the AU-1. F4U7-s were extensively employed in Indo-China against the Viet Minh.* (Vought)

wing roots and pilot armour was increased. The last AU-1 was turned over to the Marines on 10 October 1952.

Still one more Corsair variant was to be built. In response to a request from the Aeronavale, 94 F4U-7s were manufactured by Vought for the French, specifically for use in Southeast Asia. The ''-7'' was essentially identical to the cannon-armed F4U-4C. While the F4U-7 was the only Corsair specifically manufactured for a foreign power, it was by no means the only Corsair to see foreign duty. During WW2 2012 F4U-1s, -1As and -1Ds were delivered to the Royal Navy and 419 to the RNZAF. After the war, a number of South American countries operated the Corsair. The French were probably the last to fly Corsairs operationally, the last F4U-7 squadron being disbanded in 1964.

When the last F4U-7 came off Vought's assembly line in January 1953, it marked the beginning of the end of an era, not only for Vought but for naval aviation. Never again would a prop-driven fighter dominate the decks of the fleet. Still, that era had been a glorious one, punctuated by many marvellous deeds achieved in many wonderful machines. And none was more wonderful than the Corsair.

The Corsair aroused passions. Pilots who flew early models often hated the ''Hognose'' for its treacherous stalls and poor visibility. But for every critic there were many more who owed their lives to the F4U's sheer power and rugged construction, becoming passionate converts. The Corsair was never an easy bird to fly, many others were easier, but certainly no other aircraft can lay a more rightful claim to the title of ultimate propeller-driven fighting machine.

Fig. 30 *An F4U-5NL on the flight deck of* **Antietam** (Vought)

SPECIFICATIONS

XF4U-1

Dimensions: length, 31ft 11in (9728mm); span, 41ft 0in (12497mm); wing area, 314sq ft (29.2sq m).
Weights: gross weight, 9146lb (4149kg); empty weight, 7505lb (3404kg).
Performance: max speed at 16,000ft (4877m), 404mph (650km/hr); rate of climb, 2660ft/min (811m/min); range, 1000 miles (1609km); ceiling, 35,200ft (10729m).
Powerplant: Pratt & Whitney XR-2800-4 of 1850hp takeoff power.
Armament: 2×.30 (7.62mm) machine guns; 2×.50 (12.7mm) machine guns.

F4U-1A

Dimensions: length, 33ft 4in (10160mm); span, 41ft 0in (12947mm); wing area, 314sq ft (29.2sq m).
Weights: gross weight, 12,050lb (5466kg); empty weight, 8982lb (4074kg).
Performance: max speed at 16,000ft (4877m), 417mph (671km/hr); rate of climb, 3120ft/min (951m/min); range, 1015 miles (1633km); ceiling, 37,000ft (11277m).
Powerplant: Pratt & Whitney R-2800-8W of 2250hp boosted takeoff power.
Armament: 6×.50 (12.7mm) machine guns.

F4U-4

Dimensions: length, 33ft 8in (10262mm); span, 41ft 0in (12497mm); wing area, 314sq ft (29.2sq m).
Weights: gross weight, 12,250lb (5556kg); empty weight, 9205lb (4175kg).
Performance: max speed at 16,000ft (4877m), 446mph (718km/hr); rate of climb, 4000ft/min (1219m/min); range, 1000 miles (1609km); ceiling, 41,500ft (12648m).
Powerplant: Pratt & Whitney R-2800-18W of 2450hp boosted takeoff power.
Armament: 6×.50 (12.7mm) machine guns.

F4U-5

Dimensions: length, 33ft 6in (10211mm); span, 41ft 0in (12497mm); wing area, 314sq ft (29.2sq m).
Weights: gross weight, 13,000lb (5897kg); empty weight, 9835lb (4461kg).
Performance: max speed at 16,000ft (4877m), 462mph (744km/hr); rate of climb, 4230ft/min (1289m/min); range, 1030 miles (1658km); ceiling, 44,100ft (13442m).
Powerplant: Pratt & Whitney R-2800-32WE of 2450hp takeoff power.
Armament: 6×.50 (12.7mm) machine guns.

GRUMMAN F8F BEARCAT

Fig. 1 *The F8F-2s of VF-63, normally assigned to* Coral Sea, *are seen here being loaded onboard* Franklin D. Roosevelt *for exercises in the Caribbean, Norfolk, 18 February 1949.* (Grumman)

Fig. 2 *Perhaps the most persistent of the Bearcat's problems can be traced back to the original design concept and should have been obvious even in the forward fuselage mockup seen here on 10 March 1944. In an attempt to mount the biggest available engine on the smallest possible airframe, Grumman packed the maze of tubes, valves and pumps that support the Double Wasp and run the hydraulic system into too small a space between the engine and firewall, leading directly to the Bearcat's myriad maintenance problems.* (USN-NARS)

By the summer of 1943, BuAer could afford a few moments to catch its breath and reflect upon its needs. While the war in the Pacific was far from won, it was "in hand". It was unlikely that the Japanese would have any more nasty surprises, like the A6M Zero had been in 1941, that would leave the US Navy scurrying to catch up. In the F6F Hellcat and F4U Corsair, BuAer had fighters superior to anything the Japanese had in the air. But hard experience showed that the Japanese ability to design and build aircraft should not be underestimated. Certainly they were working on their next generation of fighters. Now was the time for the US to start work on the fighters to beat them.

Grumman knew the situation as well as BuAer and was determined that the Navy's new fighter would come from the same Bethpage plant that built the Wildcat and Hellcat. Therefore, in the summer of 1943, Grumman submitted its Design G-58 to the Navy. G-58 was created on the assumption that the Corsair would be the Navy's high altitude fighter for the foreseeable future, but that the Hellcat would need replacement as a low-to-medium altitude interceptor. Grumman's new design,

therefore, was optimised for best performance below 25,000ft (7620m). It was intended to pack speed, pilot protection and manoeuvrability superior to the Hellcat into an airframe the same size and weight as a Wildcat. The only sacrifice, and it was seen as a small price to pay, was a reduction from six to four .50 (12.7mm) machine guns. (The Japanese aircraft encountered so far in the war were so lightly constructed that even four .50s were considered to be more than sufficient firepower.) Power was to be supplied by a new "E"-series version (with variable speed supercharger) of the now tried and true Pratt & Whitney R-2800 Double Wasp; the same basic engine that powered the much bigger and heavier F6F and F4U.

The basic airframe of the G-58 would employ only then conventional technology. The construction was to use the skin spotwelding pioneered in the Corsair that allowed considerably lighter framing without any loss in strength. Likewise the airfoils were conventional, being the same NACA 230 series used in the F6F. A feature new to Navy aircraft, though hardly new to fighter design, was a bubble canopy allowing much better all-

Fig. 3 *The XF8F-1 underwent a brief and generally successful test programme at NATC Patuxent River. Virtually the only visible difference from production Bearcats is the lack of tail fillet, 21 September 1944.* (USN-NARS)

Fig. 4 *One of the 23 pre-production F8F-1s retained by the Navy for testing (BuNo 90447) is seen over the Maryland tidelands near NATC Patuxent River, 10 May 1945.* (NASM)

Fig. 5 *Carquals took place on* **Charger** *beginning on 17 February 1945. F8Fs were blessed with superb slow speed handling and passed these initial carrier suitability trials with flying colours* (Grumman)

round vision than possible with a Hellcat or Corsair. Lest Grumman be accused of being conservative in their design, the proposed new fighter included one absolutely revolutionary feature, break-away wingtips. The idea was actually quite simple. In order to build an aircraft that was both very fast and very manoeuvrable in the age of straight-wing aircraft called for wings with an extremely heavy structure. The result was a weight penalty that Grumman was unwilling to pay. Rather than stressing the whole wing to withstand greater than 9Gs, only the essential inner three-quarters of the span was so strong. The outer four feet of each wing were designed to deliberately fail at 9Gs and ''break-away'', leaving a shorter inner wing sufficient to get the aircraft safely home. The benefits were multiple. Mainly, it allowed a much lighter wing structure because only a shorter span had to be stressed for maximum strength. On paper, at least, ''break-away'' wingtips allowed a faster, more manoeuvrable fighter than had ever before existed.

BuAer was impressed. On 27 November 1943, two prototypes of the XF8F-1 Bearcat, as the new fighter was designated, were ordered. The first of these, BuNo 90460, was ready on 31 August 1944 and flew on that date. The only change from original plans was in the powerplant. The ''E''-series Double Wasp was taking

longer to develop than anticipated and was replaced by an R-2800-22W with conventional two-speed super-charger. The engine provided 2100hp for takeoff and allowed the Bearcat to reach 424mph (682km/hr) at 17,300ft (5273m) and climb at 4,800ft/min (1463m/min). Actually, the replacement engine caused little loss in performance and, when the Navy pronounced itself satisfied with the prototype, the initial production models were ordered with the nearly identical R-2800-34WA, the ''E''-series engine still being unavailable.

Initial flight tests of the first prototype was nearly uniformly successful. Very few problems seemed to crop up. By mid-October, BuAer felt the Bearcat was ready to be demonstrated and decided to ''unveil'' the first prototype at a Joint Fighter Conference being held at NATC Patuxent River. In informal competition against the best new fighters of the Army and Navy, the Bearcat stood out. It was adjudged the best fighter under 25,000ft (7620m) in an informal ''straw poll''. The Navy was confident that it had a winner in the Bearcat and did not even wait for the conference to place its initial production order. 2023 F8F-1s, including 23 pre-production models, were ordered from Grumman on 6 October 1944.

Fig. 6 *'K21', an early F8F-1 sits on the flight deck of a light carrier in the immediate postwar period. This markings scheme, with yellow lettering and white-only national insignia was official only between June 1946 and January 1947, when the red stripe was authorised for the 'star-and-bar'.* (NASM)

Fig. 7 *A new markings scheme was introduced in January 1947, at the same time that Bearcats began to arrive in the fleet in large numbers. Here F8F-1s of VF-11 display those markings. Squadrons were renumbered to indicate their position in the Carrier Air Group – VF-11 was the first squadron in CVG-1 (the second was VF-12, etc.) All aircraft now carried a three number code, the first number representing the squadron, the second and third the position within the squadron. The tail letter indicated air group rather than carrier, although the original letter assignments were related to the name of the ship on which it was serving in January 1947, CVG-1 was assigned to Tarawa during this period.(USN)*

The only complaints heard during initial testing were about excessive fuel consumption causing shorter than specified range and about longitudinal instability. The first problem was to be solved by an increase in internal fuel capacity from 150 to 183gal (568 to 693lt), the second by the addition of a dorsal fillet to the vertical tail. These changes were made in the second prototype (BuNo 90438) and test flown in late 1944. The Bearcat's range was now considered satisfactory. Stability was improved though still less than optimal. Still, BuAer was sure that the Bearcat was significantly superior to the Hellcat ''as is'' and began to lay plans for the phasing out of F6F and FM2(F4F) production in favour of the F8F. Eastern's projected Wildcat upgrade, the F2M, was rejected. Instead, Eastern was contracted for 1876

F3M-1s(F8F-1s) on 5 February 1945. Production from Bethpage was to reach 100 Bearcats per month in June 1945 and total phase out of Hellcat production was to occur in January 1946. Eastern was to join in as soon as tooling could be set up.

The Bearcat programme proceeded at top speed despite the fact that the war situation was now markedly changed from the time of the fighter's inception. Carquals began on 17 February 1945 on *Charger* and were completed rapidly and successfully. The first Bearcat squadron, VF-19, formed at NAS Santa Rosa on 21 May. The Navy was eager to get their new fighter into service before the war wound down. Even the loss of the first prototype in a crash in March failed to slow

Fig. 8 *CVLG-1 served on Saipan, hence the 'SA' tailcode for that air group. Each of the F8F-1s here carries a near maximum external load, two 5" (127mm) HVARs and a 100lb (45kg) bomb under each wing. (NASM)*

Fig. 9 *The only thing more embarrassing than landing on the wrong carrier was having to clean up the mess when you got home. This F8F-1 of* **Leyte's** *VF-10A landed on* **Kearsarge** *by mistake and received the traditional paint job before it was allowed to return, 25 Sept 1947.* (USN-NARS)

the pace. However, VF-19 began to experience some problems with their new mount stemming directly from the haste with which the Bearcat was being introduced. A series of engine failures, both in flight and at takeoff, began to plague the F8F-1. The failures were linked to two separate causes. The takeoff failures were blamed specifically on insufficient ground run-up and were cured by lengthening the warm-up period before flight. The in flight failures were blamed on the use of a too-lean fuel mixture and were solved by a richer cruise setting on the throttle. (This in turn led to excessive spark plug fouling which bedevilled the Bearcat throughout its career.) More generally, the Bearcat was found to suffer from a spate of fuel leaks and seal failures in the complex maze of lines, tubes and wires between the engine and firewall. In their great desire to produce the smallest possible aircraft, Grumman had tried to pack all of the plumbing for the Double Wasp into too small an area. The result was a servicing nightmare that was never satisfactorily solved. A small but steady number of landing gear failures were also being reported. Further investigation turned up leaks in the hydraulic system. And pilots continued to complain about the directional stability.

At one point in mid-1945, the maintenance problems with the Bearcat became so severe that BuAer was forced to ground all F8Fs, but pressure to get the new fighter into combat was so great that the ban was soon lifted and VF-19 was back in the air again. That squadron flew its carquals on *Takanis Bay* in mid-July and was declared combat ready. VF-19 embarked on *Langley* on 2 August 1945, enroute to the war zone. Meanwhile, the second Bearcat squadron, VF-18, began forming at NAS North Island.

Although BuAer intended to let nothing interfere with its determination to see Bearcats in combat, it could not ignore the continuing handling problems of the new fighter. Therefore, in mid-1945 an F8F-1 was turned over to NACA at Langley Field for exhaustive flight and full-scale windtunnel tests. The results were certainly not unexpected. NACA found that the Bearcat's instability was the result of hanging too powerful an engine on too small an airframe and could only be remedied by increasing flight surface area. Specifically, they recommended increasing the height of the vertical tail by 16in (406mm). BuAer turned this finding over to Grumman with instructions to make the necessary design alterations but to introduce the change only at model changeover to the ''E''-series-powered F8F-2. (Development of this much-delayed Double Wasp variant was still expected to be completed in the near future.)

Fig. 10 *Coming in 'high and hot', this F8F-1 of* **Valley Forge**'s *VF-111 appears to be headed for the barrier, 29 March 1948.* (USN)

The surrender of Japan was a cause for worldwide jubilation, although the joy must have been tinged with regret at Grumman, Eastern and onboard *Langley*. At war's end, Grumman's contract was pared down to 770 Bearcats, including those already delivered. Production set at 100 per month was to be reduced to 15. Eastern fared even worse, their entire Bearcat order being cancelled. VF-19 had cause for sorrow as well. Despite everyone's best efforts, they arrived in the western Pacific too late to see action.

War's end seemed to leave the F8F securely cast in the role of the Navy's primary low-to-medium altitude dogfighter. But such a situation was to be only temporary at best. The Bearcat's future was already clouded. Handling and hydraulic problems continued to plague the Bearcats then entering service in increasing numbers. (A postwar report assured BuAer that while the main hydraulic system was prone to periodic failure, the emergency landing gear extension system was 100% reliable.) More so than the Corsair, the Bearcat's service career was threatened by the jets just coming off US drawing boards. This was because the projected early jets, specifically the FJ Fury and FD Phantom, would possess much the same characteristics as the F8F but in

greater measure. Like the Bearcat, they were to be short range, highly manoeuvrable, lightly loaded dogfighters. (The Corsair, because of its long range, high altitude performance and load carrying ability, was less likely to be immediately threatened by the new jets.)

The Bearcat still played a major role in BuAer's postwar plans. Among the decisions made at war's end was that henceforth a quarter of all Bearcat's would be armed with four 20mm cannons in the place of the .50s. (On 27 March 1946, the cannon-armed Bearcat was designated F8F-1B.) Priority was given to introducing the ''E''-series engine, now named R-2800-30W, into service. All Bearcat development was put on hold in December 1945, however, when the first fatal crash of an F8F occurred. The cause was the ''break-away'' of one wingtip during low altitude manoeuvres. The assumption had been that both wingtips would fail at the same time. This accident showed that such an assumption could not in fact be made, and further that the suddenly uneven forces caused by the loss of one wingtip could be controlled only if the pilot had plenty of altitude in which to recover. Such a failure at low altitude was an invitation to disaster. Investigation showed that there were inconsistencies in the strength of the joint of the "break-away" section and the rest of the wing that might cause an asymmetrical failure. Starting with the 251st example, Bearcats came off the line with a revised bolt arrangement at the joint and with strengthened wing roots.

In the late spring of 1946, a Bearcat flew mock combat with an FO-1 (a navalized P-80). The outcome was even worse than expected. The Bearcat's pilot complained that he had been unable to gain even one good "set-up" on the jet, which was consistently able to outmanoeuvre and outaccelerate the prop. BuAer understood the implications, as did Grumman. F8Fs remained in production only because development of the first naval jets was taking longer than expected. Despite the fact that everyone knew that the Bearcat was now a stopgap fighter, the number of VFs flying the Bearcat had increased to nine by the end of the year.

In late 1946, the XF8F-2 (BuNo 95049) finally took to the air. The prototype was powered by a pre-production model of the 2250hp, variable-speed super-charged R-2800-30W and easily reached 447mph (719km/hr) at 28,000ft (8534m) making it the fastest military Bearcat. Rate of climb reached an astounding 6600ft/min (2012m/min). Standard armament was four 20mm cannons. The XF8F-2 incorporated the enlarged vertical tail that had been suggested a year earlier by NACA. It was extended by 12in (305mm), rather than the recommended 16in (406mm), because that was the greatest enlargement considered possible without a total redesign of the tail structure. It appeared to be sufficient. Test pilots reported that the stability problems were reduced to the point of insignificance. The prototype also included a further attempt to prevent the possibility of asymmetrical wingtip "break-away". Electrically actuated explosive bolts were installed at the joint, so that the pilot could rapidly restore symmetry if only one wingtip separated. (Even this proved to be an inadequate precaution. At least one more fatal accident occurred when one wingtip "broke-away" at low altitude and the aircraft crashed before the pilot had a chance to actuate the explosive bolts. Finally, in 1950, all Bearcats had the "break-away" wingtips removed and replaced by normal, permament wingtips.)

Successful flight testing on the XF8F-2 continued into 1947. Because the projected F8F-2 was essentially similar to the F8F-1B, except for tail and powerplant, BuAer decided to phase out the F8F-1 immediately in favour of the -1B and to phase in the F8F-2 as soon as R-2800-30Ws were available in quantity. F8F-1 production ceased after the delivery of the 770th example. Continued delays in jet delivery led to a further increase in squadron service for the Bearcat. At the end of 1947, 19 squadrons flew the F8F-1 and four more were equipped with F8F-1Bs. Late in the year, however, the first FD-1s and FJs entered fleet service.

Fig. 11 *This F8F-1B (BuNo 122110 — note the cannon barrels) prepares to take off from* Leyte. *On 1 May 1948, a system of colour coded tailtips and prop hubs was introduced to further distinguish a carrier's squadrons. As the second squadron in CVG-7, VF-72's Bearcats carried white trim.* (NASM)

Fig. 12 *A number of Bearcats were converted to drone control aircraft. The first F8F-1D (BuNo 90446) displays the markings of NADC Johnsville, where this variant was developed.* (NASM)

(In June 1947, Grumman delivered a single F8F-1 to a civilian owner, Gulf Oil Co, with the full approval of the Navy. The G-58A Gulfhawk 4th (civil registration NL3025) continued the glorious tradition of the three previous orange and blue Gulfhawks and began a new tradition of Bearcats as demonstration and racing aircraft. 1300lbs (590kg) lighter than its military counterpart and powered by a civilianised R-2800-22 capable of delivering 2800hp in bursts, the G-58A reportedly could maintain 500mph (805km/hr) in level flight at 19,000ft (5791m). Very popular with airshow crowds, the Gulfhawk 4th unfortunately had a very short career, being demolished in a landing accident in 1948. When Gulf chose not to replace the G-58A, Grumman decided to step in and got Navy approval to similarly modify an F8F-2 into the G-58 (civil registration N700A) demonstration and test aircraft.)

Continually delayed by development problems, the R-2800-30W finally reached Grumman assembly lines in quantity in January 1948 and F8F-1B production was phased out in favour of the F8F-2 after 126-1Bs had been completed. Late in that year, the number of Bearcat squadrons reached a peak of 24 but began to decline rapidly as F8F-1s began to be passed on to the Reserves. Production of the F8F-2 ended in May 1949 after 293

were built.

With "first generation" jets re-equipping many fleet VFs and "second generation" F2H Banshees and F9F Panthers beginning to arrive, the service life of the F8F-2 was bound to be short. When war broke out in Korea in 1950, the Navy decided not to commit Bearcats to combat. It no longer was the Navy's premier interceptor nor could it carry loads like the Corsair. It certainly appeared as if this diminutive dogfighter was fated never to fire its guns in anger. On 5 June 1950, the F8F-1 officially replaced the Hellcat as the Navy's principal advanced trainer.

Bearcats did indeed see combat, though not in US markings. In 1954, the French Aeronavale was given 100 F8F-1s and F8F-1Bs for use in Indo-China against the Vietminh. There they were continually engaged in ground support operations from land bases until the fall of Dien Bien Phu. After the French evacuated Vietnam, the remaining Aeronavale Bearcats were turned over to the South Vietnamese, equipping the RVNAF's 514th FS. At the same time, 29 Bearcats were delivered to Thailand for use in their continual struggle against insurgents. They were employed by the Thais, while carrying the most colourful markings that ever graced F8Fs, well into the 1960s.

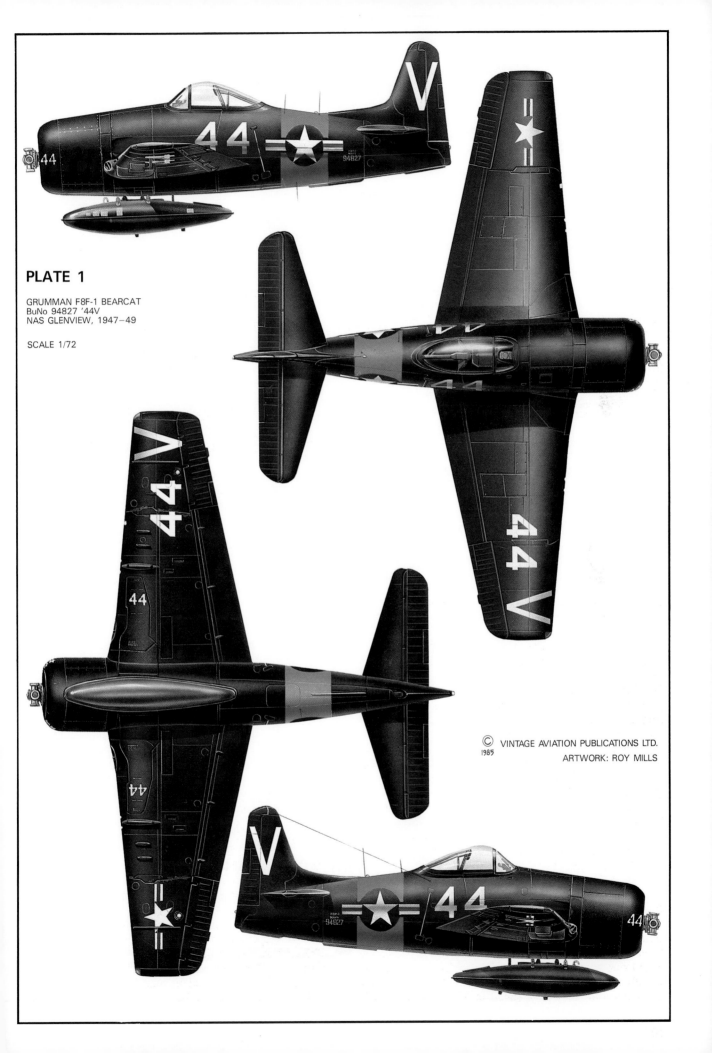

PLATE 1

GRUMMAN F8F-1 BEARCAT
BuNo 94827 '44V
NAS GLENVIEW, 1947—49

SCALE 1/72

© VINTAGE AVIATION PUBLICATIONS LTD.
1985
ARTWORK: ROY MILLS

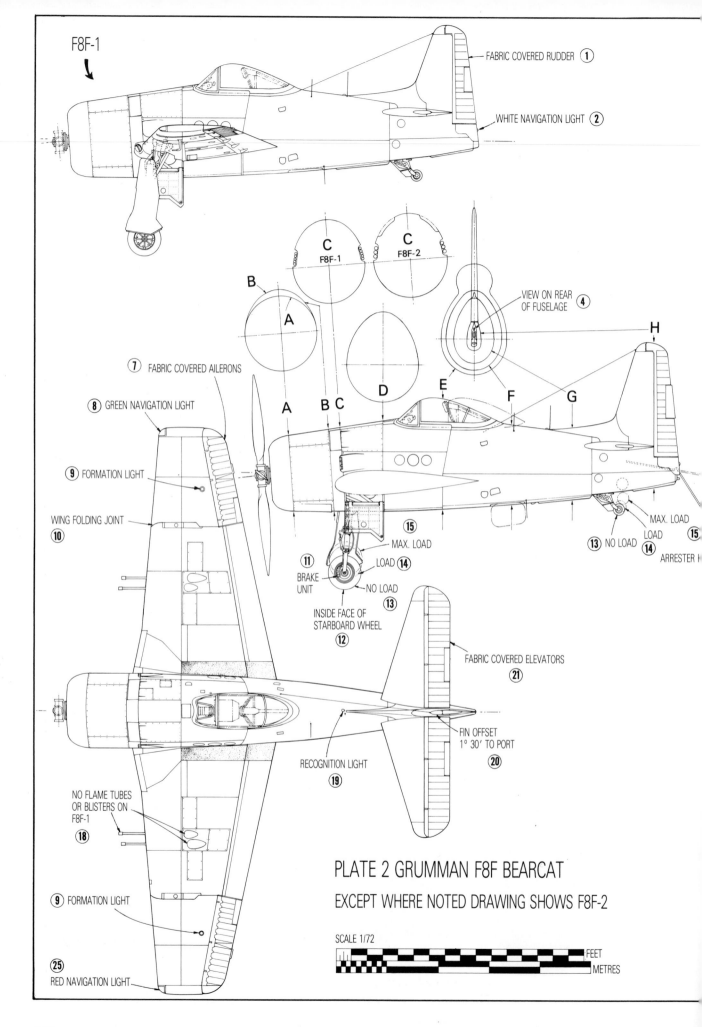

F8F-1

FABRIC COVERED RUDDER (1)

WHITE NAVIGATION LIGHT (2)

C
F8F-1

C
F8F-2

B

A

A   B C

VIEW ON REAR
OF FUSELAGE (4)

H

D

E

F   G

(7) FABRIC COVERED AILERONS

(8) GREEN NAVIGATION LIGHT

(9) FORMATION LIGHT

WING FOLDING JOINT
(10)

(15)

MAX. LOAD

MAX. LOAD

(13) NO LOAD   LOAD
(14)   (15)

ARRESTER H

MAX. LOAD

(11)
BRAKE
UNIT

LOAD (14)

NO LOAD

(13)

INSIDE FACE OF
STARBOARD WHEEL
(12)

FABRIC COVERED ELEVATORS

(21)

FIN OFFSET
1° 30' TO PORT

(20)

RECOGNITION LIGHT

(19)

NO FLAME TUBES
OR BLISTERS ON
F8F-1

(18)

(9) FORMATION LIGHT

PLATE 2 GRUMMAN F8F BEARCAT

EXCEPT WHERE NOTED DRAWING SHOWS F8F-2

SCALE 1/72

FEET
METRES

(25)
RED NAVIGATION LIGHT

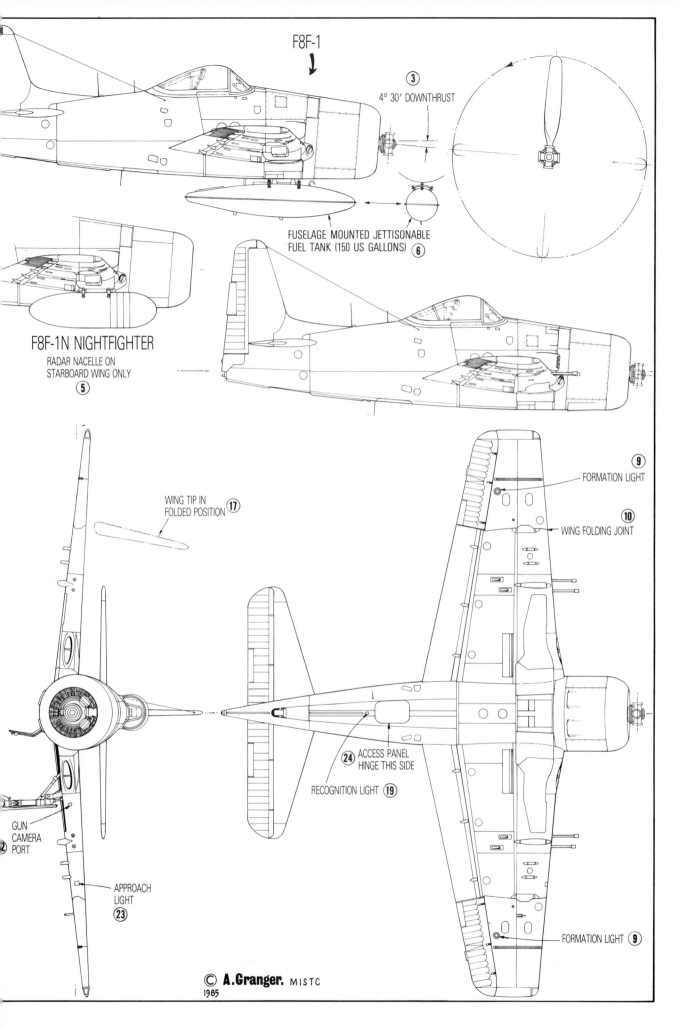

F8F-1

③ 4° 30' DOWNTHRUST

FUSELAGE MOUNTED JETTISONABLE
FUEL TANK (150 US GALLONS) ⑥

F8F-1N NIGHTFIGHTER

RADAR NACELLE ON
STARBOARD WING ONLY
⑤

WING TIP IN
FOLDED POSITION ⑰

⑨ FORMATION LIGHT

⑩ WING FOLDING JOINT

GUN
CAMERA
PORT

㉔ ACCESS PANEL
HINGE THIS SIDE

RECOGNITION LIGHT ⑲

APPROACH
LIGHT
㉓

FORMATION LIGHT ⑨

© A. Granger. MISTC
1985

PLATE 3   UNIT MARKINGS   SCALE 1/72

① F8F-1 '101S, USS *SHANGRI LA*, 1948-49

② G-58A (F8F-1) NL3025
GULFHAWK 4th, AL WILLIAMS, 1947

③ MARKINGS ON UPPER &
LOWER SURFACES

⑤ F8F-2 BuNo 121565
'210D OF VF-29
USS *LEYTE*, JUNE 1949

GRUMMAN COMPANY
EMBLEM ON
GULFHAWK
FIN
④

⑥ F8F-2 BuNo 121553
'553 MCAS QUANTICO,
27 JULY 1951

⑦ F8F-2D, BuNo 121782
'68 UD, c.1955

ARTWORK:
ROY MILLS

© VINTAGE AVIATION PUBLICATIONS LTD.
1985

Fig. 13 *The Blue Angels flew Bearcats from August 1946 until June 1949, but this view must date from 1949 because the name was carried on the cowling only in that year. The group loved the Bearcat's acceleration and manoeuvreability but did not miss the big prop when they traded them in on Panthers.* (NASM)

Fig. 14 *A number of F8F-1s were assigned to test duties after they were retired from front-line service, including BuNo 94759 which was employed by NAF-NO TS (Naval Air Facility – Naval Ordnance Test Station) Inyokern. It is seen at Edwards AFB in May 1950 in the 'HiVi 2' scheme of overall sea blue with chrome yellow wings.* (Jim Sullivan)

Fig. 15 *One of the two XF8F-2s (BuNo 95049 – a converted F8F-1) is seen at NATC Patuxent River on 18 July 1949. It has the extended tail but lacks the cannon armament of the production F8F-2.* (NHC)

Fig. 16 *F8F-2s rapidly replaced F8F-1s in the fleet. This example was assigned to VF-72 on* **Leyte.** (Jim Sullivan)

Fig. 17. Above   *Two squadrons of F8F-2s of CVG-15 are loaded onboard an unidentified carrier already having two squadrons of CVG-19's ADs on deck. In the background are the Bearcats of VF-152. A red-trimmed F8F-2s of VF-151 is being loaded, another sits in the foreground. Of interest is the striped decoration, probably yellow and red, on the rudder trim tab and tailcone of the VF-151 birds.* (Grumman)

Fig. 18. Below   *The Marines got a few Bearcats in 1951. A pair of F8F-2s (BuNo 121540 in the foreground) are seen in the markings of MCAS Quantico, 27 June 1951.* (NASM)

Fig. 19. Above *Twelve F8F-2s were fitted with APS-19 radar and flash hiders for the cannons and redesignated F8F-2Ns.* (USN)

Fig. 20. Below *A small number of F8F-2Ds were created by modifying standard F8F-2s as drone controllers. The High Visibility scheme now included chrome yellow tail and wings with red rudder and wing stripe. BuNo 121782 is seen in a boneyard awaiting disposal.* (Jim Sullivan)

Fig. 21. Above *As Bearcats were turned over to the Reserves, they began to sport markings that could easily be confused with those of fleet units, were it not for the broad orange stripe around the fuselage. The 'V' on this F8F-1 (BuNo 94850) indicates NAS Glenview rather than CVG-11 off* **Valley Forge**. *The national insignia centred on the orange stripe dates this view from the period 1947–1949.* (NASM)

Fig. 22. Below *Another Reserve F8F-1 (BuNo 94842) is seen after 1949 when the national insignia was moved forward of the band, being replaced by 'NAVY' and the name of the station, in this case NAS Anacostia. (Though it is virtually impossible to see because this photo was taken with or-thochromatic film which turns orange dark, the orange band is there.)* (NASM)

Fig. 23   *F8F-2s were turned over to the Reserves after 1950. BuNo 121619 of the Denver Reserves is seen at NAS Glenview in March 1952.*   (Clay Jansson via Jim Sullivan)

Fig. 24. Above *Bearcats replaced Hellcats as the Navy's main advanced trainer in 1950. A trio of F8F-1s of ATU-2 from NAS Corpus Christi are seen on 25 April 1951.* (NASM)

Fig. 25. Below *Eight of ATU-100's F8F-1s are seen in flight in 1953. Even as a flight trainer Bearcats did not last long, being replaced by jet trainers as soon as they became available.* (USN)

Fig. 26 *N700A was an F8F-2 flown by Grumman for test and for publicity purposes. It performed many of the same airshow routines as the short-lived Gulfhawk 4th.* (NASM)

In late 1955, the last US Navy Bearcats were retired from reserve service and placed in storage at NAS Litchfield Park and North Island. 50 more were sent to the French and a number more were sold off to civilians for conversion into racers, the remainder were scrapped in 1958-9.

It was as a racer that the Bearcat had its last brief moment of glory. In 1969, Darryl Greenamayer took his much modified F8F-2 (ex-BuNo121646, civil registration N111L) to a new official propeller aircraft speed record (480mph) (772km/hr) at Edwards AFB, beating the record held by the Bf 209 for 30 years.

The Bearcat was a aircraft that truly was in the wrong place at the wrong time. Had it been ready even a year earlier, it would have stood out among the great interceptors of WW2. As it was, it arrived in time to witness the end but not help achieve it. By the time American guns were next firing in anger, Bearcats were in the process of being retired from front-line service and again F8Fs watched history without influencing it. If not a brilliant design, the Bearcat certainly was a worthy successor to the preceeding Bethpage "cats", and no doubt would have, had it had the chance, earned a reputation as great as its potential.

Fig. 27 *Darryl Greenamayer broke the prop air speed record held by the Bf 209 since 1939 in this highly modified F8F-2 (ex-BuNo 121646).*

Fig. 28 & 29 *F8F-1 of CV38 on* **Shangri La,** *with wing mounted Mitchell motion camera pod.* **February 1946.** (USN/NARS)

SPECIFICATIONS

XF8F-1

Dimensions: length, 27ft 8in (8433mm); span, 35ft 6in (10820mm); wing area, 244sq ft (22.7sq m).
Weights: gross weight, 8800lb (3992kg); empty weight, 7017lb (3183kg).
Performance: max speed at 17,300ft (5273m), 424mph (682km/hr) rate of climb, 4800ft/min (1463m/min); range, 1000 miles (1609km); ceiling, 33,700ft (10271m).
Powerplant: Pratt & Whitney R-2800-22W of 2100hp takeoff power.
Armament: 4×.50 (12.7mm) machine guns.

F8F-1

Dimensions: length, 27ft 8in (8433mm); span, 35ft 6in (10820mm); wing area, 244sq ft (22.7sq m).
Weights: gross weight, 9600lb (4355kg); empty weight, 7170lb (3183kg).
Performance: max speed at 19,700ft (6004m), 421mph (678km/hr) rate of climb, 4800ft/min (1463m/min); range, 1140 miles (1835km); ceiling, 38,900ft (11856m).
Powerplant: Pratt & Whitney R-2800-34W of 2100hp takeoff power.
Armament: 4×.50 (12.7mm) machine guns (4×20mm cannon in F8F-1B).

F8F-2

Dimensions: length, 27ft 6in (8382mm); span, 35ft 6in (10820mm); wing area, 244sq ft (22.7sq m).
Weights: gross weight, 10,400lb (4717kg); empty weight, 7650lb (3470kg).
Performance: max speed at 28,000ft (8534m), 447mph (719km/hr) rate of climb, 6600ft/min (2012m/min); range, 1100 miles (1770km); ceiling, 40,700ft (12405m).
Powerplant: Pratt & Whitney R-2800-30W of 2250hp takeoff power.
Armament: 4×20mm cannon.